THE NEW
COMPLEAT IMBIBER

OTHER BOOKS BY
OR EDITED BY
CYRIL RAY

ON WINE AND KINDRED SUBJECTS

The Gourmet's Companion (edited with introduction)
The Compleat Imbiber: Nos 1—12 (edited, 1956–71)
Morton Shand's A Book of French Wines (revised and edited)
In a Glass Lightly
Lafite: The Story of Château Lafite-Rothschild
Mouton-Rothschild: The Wine, the Family, the Museum
Bollinger: Story of a Champagne
Cognac
Wine with Food (with Elizabeth Ray)
The Wines of Italy
The Wines of France
The Wines of Germany
The Complete Book of Spirits and Liqueurs
The St Michael Guide to Wine
Ray on Wine
Lickerish Limericks, with filthy pictures by Charles Mozley
The New Book of Italian Wines
Robert Mondavi of the Napa Valley
and sponsored works on Ruffino Chianti, Warre's Port,
the Bartons of Langoa and Léoville, etc.

ON OTHER SUBJECTS

Scenes and Characters from Surtees
Algiers to Austria: 78 Division in the Second World War
The Pageant of London
Merry England
Regiment of the Line: The Story of the Lancashire Fusiliers
Best Murder Stories (edited, with introduction)

THE NEW
COMPLEAT IMBIBER

edited by Cyril Ray

COLLINS
8 Grafton Street, London W1
1986

William Collins Sons & Co. Ltd
London . Glasgow . Sydney . Auckland
Toronto . Johannesburg

Designed by Bob Vickers
Produced by The Bowerdean Press Ltd., London SW11

British Library Cataloguing in Publication Data
The New compleat imbiber.
1. Food habits   2. Wine—social aspects
1. Ray, Cyril
394.1′2   GT2860
ISBN 0-00-217704-8

First published 1986
© Selection and arrangement of material Cyril Ray 1986
© This edition Bowerdean Press 1986
© 'Rumpole and the Blind Tasting' Advanpress Ltd., 1986

Typeset by TJB Photosetting Ltd., South Witham, Lincolnshire

Made and printed in Great Britain by
R.J. Acford Ltd., Chichester, Sussex

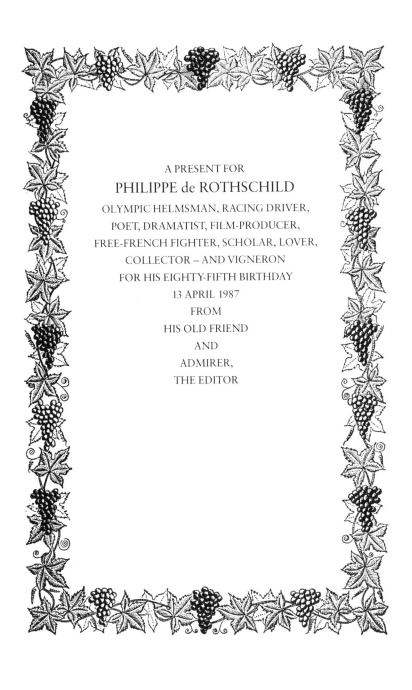

A PRESENT FOR
PHILIPPE de ROTHSCHILD
OLYMPIC HELMSMAN, RACING DRIVER,
POET, DRAMATIST, FILM-PRODUCER,
FREE-FRENCH FIGHTER, SCHOLAR, LOVER,
COLLECTOR – AND VIGNERON
FOR HIS EIGHTY-FIFTH BIRTHDAY
13 APRIL 1987
FROM
HIS OLD FRIEND
AND
ADMIRER,
THE EDITOR

Contents

Introduction   *John Arlott*   9
Editorial Postscript   13
As a Sort of Hors d'Oeuvre...   16

A Vintner's View...   19
....a Consumer's...Mr Pooter's Letter   *Keith Waterhouse*   24
....and a Diner's-Out...'Life is Beautiful'   *Edith Templeton*   28
Mrs Beeton and Mrs Dickens   *Margaret Lane*   33
The Sixty-Year Old Solitary Chez Soi   *Iris Murdoch*   39
Bingo for Bifteck: Lotto in the Lot   *Ruth Silvestre*   44
Investing in Futures: a Story   *Kingsley Amis*   47
Rumpole and the Blind Tasting: a Story   *John Mortimer*   57
Sherry: a Story   *Peter Fleming*   67
The Three Low Masses: a Christmas Story
        Alphonse Daudet   76
Beats to the Bar   *Roger Woddis*   85
'The Dons on the Dais Serene'   *Roger Lewis*   87
Drinker to Lover, Drunkard to Lecher   *Gavin Ewart*   92

SOME PEOPLE

Carlo, Portrait of a Maître d'Hôtel   *Cyril Ray*   94
Gastronomer Royal   *Christopher Driver*   97
How to Succeed at the Bar   *Cyril Ray*   106
Have It Your Way   *Elizabeth David*   108

A PHILIPPE DE ROTHSCHILD DIPTYCH

I. Mouton, 1918: 'My Idea of Paradise'
   Baron Philippe de Rothschild   114
II. The Napa Valley, 1980: Entente Cordiale   *Cyril Ray*   119

THREE PLATES OF PASTA

Pasta? Basta!   *Paul Dehn*   130
'I Like All Simple Things'   *Somerset Maugham*   132
How To Do It   *Norman Lewis*   134

Madame Poulard's Secret   *Elizabeth David*   138
Wine and/or Women   *Peter Dickinson*   140
The Boom in Beaumes   *Robin and Judith Yapp*   142
Wine in General   *Sir John Hackett*   145

ON THE HOUSE

Front Bench Looks Back   *Roy Hattersley*   152
Liberal Sees Red   *Clement Freud*   155
The Tipplings of a Travelling Tory   *Julian Critchley*   158

SOME MEMORABLE MEALS

It Isn't Only Peaches Down in Georgia   *Harry Luke*   164
Victorian Dinner-Party   *E F Benson*   166
Corporate Luncheon   *Roy Fuller*   171
Returning to the Sauce...   *Bernard Levin*   172
A McGonagall-type Triolet   *Gavin Ewart*   176

Good Health!   *Cyril Ray*   177
Two Harvests in Tuscany   *Elizabeth Romer*   181
    October: Vintage
    December: Olive Harvest
Two Brandies: Two Countries   *Elizabeth Ray*   193

BREAKFASTS AND BREAKFASTS

'A Scanty Fork Breakfast'   *R S Surtees*   202
Matter for a May Morning   *Thomas Love Peacock*   204
Awful Warning   *George Augustus Sala*   205

The Incompleat Teetotaller
    William McGonagall Unmasked   207
What to Buy and What to Drink in 1987
    Edmund Penning-Rowsell   211

Notes on some Contributors   218
The Illustrators   223
Acknowledgements   224

Introduction

John Arlott

S o, we have another *Compleat Imbiber*, always a cordial matter. It is, though, sad for the older addicts to find it called 'New', for the *Compleat Imbiber* – Cyril Ray's *Imbiber* – is 30 years and, with this, 13 numbers, old. Perhaps, though, the editor is superstitious.

Many who pick up this volume will recall the first of the species, dated 1956, with its arresting dust-wrapper by Hoffnung, typical of him, who was unique among comic artists. To mention him is to realize that, among the contributors to that original collection, some other master hands were no longer available for this issue. First among them, in wine terms surely, must be Raymond Postgate who imparted a fresh and clear-cut attitude to English writing on the subject. Then, we may raise a compulsive, and appropriate, glass to Sir John Betjeman, Sir Alan Herbert, Patrick Campbell, Kenneth Tynan, and Sir Compton Mackenzie. Still, though, the editor can call, from that first volume, upon himself, Iris Murdoch and, and, and – O Gawd!

That first *Imbiber* had a mixed career. It was the kind of book that has always attracted publishers; and the first collection – published by Putnam – ran to a second (1957) edition which prompted a *Compleat Imbiber* No 2 in 1958. It was to know three more publishers before what seemed long to be the final volume, in 1971. That, too, had a piece by Raymond Postgate; a poem 'To the Widow Clicquot' by no less than Robert Nichols; articles by Alan Coren, Anthony Powell, René Cutforth and Derek Cooper; but the Hutchinson axe descended.

After that, it seemed that the title – series – idea – had died the death. Something or other – can never remember what it is – will always, they say, rise to the top; and gradually – in about 1980 – odd volumes of it began to appear in booksellers' catalogues at about £5 each and increase steadily in scarcity and rise upwards in price. (The first six *Imbibers* had been published at twenty-five shillings each; then three at thirty shillings; one at £2.25; one at £2.50; No. 12 was £3.50)

The collectors were at work; so, sensing quality, were the growing body of what I suppose I must call wine-readers. Perhaps the most important point to me in this, the now 'antiquarian' *Imbiber*'s progress, was when a distinguished London antiquarian bookseller told me, just before Christmas 1985, that she had sold a complete twelve-volume run the year before for £250 within a couple of days of putting it in the window: this Christmas, she said, she'd be lucky to find a set that would bring her a profit at £300.

Thus was the editor's choice vindicated in the ultimate market of history: but it is important that he is still at hand to demonstrate the taste and judgement that created the previous series. It is important that Cyril Ray does not regard himself as a complete and final authority on the subject. He learned about wine primarily through drinking it because he enjoyed it; then through his contacts with the people who grew the grapes and made the wine; then, because he was always a sound scholar, through reading in the subject. Always, though, his attitude to wine has been governed by interested pleasure in drinking it, in writing about it with humanity, and a spice of humour.

In a way – no, in fact – the history of *The Compleat Imbiber* reflects the modern history of wine-drinking in Britain. The post-1945 increase in the British consumption of wine by service-men returning from the war in Europe began to spread out beyond the privileged *grand-cru*-only customers of the establishment wine merchants to the predominantly literate class previously, apparently and mysteriously, socially debarred from it. Continental tourism and the package holiday continued the popularization of wine begun, in their different fashions, by André Simon and Tommy Layton before 1939.

Now, it is not only easy, but accurate, to say that, in the 'natural' wine-drinking countries, most people have found no need to read about the commodity. The British, however, had much to learn; far more, obviously, than the people of most of the wine-producing countries. It is not uncommon in Burgundy to find a shop selling Burgundy wines, but none from Bordeaux; and *vice versa* – though this grows increasingly rare – probably – or at least possibly – because of the British influence. French wines are considered – not only by the French – the finest in the world. Yet the truth is that British shops can show a far greater variety of the wines of the world, if only because, they would suggest, they are not parochial, because they have no overriding loyalty; the French would argue that *their* attitude is the ultimate degree of discrimination – or, at least, loyalty.

So here was the classic dilemma; or if not classic, the basis for the old story of the all-rounder and the specialist. In short, the producing countries of Europe are highly expert in the making, tasting and history of their own local wines; on the other hand, the British open their markets to the vineyards of the world. This statement demands apologies on behalf of the reviving production of English wines. (Alas that they are bedevilled, in so many minds, by the so-called 'British' wines, which are not British at all nor, by strict definition, wines, either.)

The French produce fine, indeed distinguished periodicals and books on the subject but they are blinkeredly French. The Americans – not solely as a hobby, nor only in California – are wine-makers who also drink through a wide range across the world; though their immense predilection for Lambrusco casts doubts on their majority palates. The Australians, too, have lately branched out beyond the vineyards of the early German settlers to swap rail containers of wine to balance each other's deficiencies and excesses; and a growing sector there finds an interest in wine in general.

It is in Britain, though, that the greatest modern conversion has taken place. Perhaps it is a British characteristic that, side by side with the growth in wine-drinking, a read-about-it attitude has grown up. It must surely be significant that the first planning of this book coincided with an unparalleled growth in the number not only of specialist wine bookshops, but dealers in wine antiques and artefacts, wine prints, tutored tastings and at a time when three British wine periodicals could healthily coexist.

This *Imbiber* reflects, too, the growing interest in gastronomy in general; surely a healthy sign; healthy enough, indeed, to make its missionary to Britain, André Simon, turn contentedly in his grave with a mixture of both amazement and delight.

If some of the old familiar faces of the first volume have gone, others of distinction have taken their places. It is always an immense delight to encounter Elizabeth David anywhere, in the flesh or print; in many ways she has done for British cooking what André Simon and Raymond Postgate did for our wine-drinking; and, that apart, she is such a polished writer. The editor's providential sense of humour – without which an English wine collection would be in danger of wine-snobbery – admits the two quite surgically precise pieces of debunking – one personal, one gastronomic – in verse, by Gavin Ewart. Robin Yapp continues his faithful Rhône missionary work – next time, no doubt it will be Loire. It would be stupid to suggest that Edmund Penning-Rowsell, our pre-eminent Bordeaux scholar, was not a familiar figure to old *Imbiber* habitués but, while he missed the first of the few, he was building up his fuel for many issues to come. Keith Waterhouse has unearthed a jewel of Pooterism about the famous Jackson champagne; while Kingsley Amis produces another of his salutary correctives to wine solemnity. Thus, once more, the editor has produced a small, but balanced, cellar of delights – and the beginning of another run of *Imbibers*?

Alderney, 1986

Editorial Postscript

I T is a considerable pleasure for an editor to have a new omnium gatherum introduced by a contributor – by no means the least distinguished one, either – to the first of its forerunners, published thirty years before.

John Arlott's 1956 essay, *At the Sign of the Bat and Ball*, was fashioned out of two of what were then, and are still, his multifarious enthusiasms – cricket and good living. He dipped delightedly and delightfully into the bills of fare, the toast lists and the minute books of the Bat and Ball Inn on Broadhalfpenny Down, where cricket was born and 'where those legendary Hampshire village cricketers met on the first Tuesday of every May for more than fifty great summers.' I was tempted to reprint the whole evocative and essentially English piece of inspired prose, but this is the *New* 'Compleat Imbiber' and I must not cheat, but content myself and tantalize my readers with merely two of John's quotations from *The Cricketers of My Time* (c.1830) by the landlord's son, John Nyren, himself according to the DNB, 'a left-handed batsman of average ability and a fine field at point and middle wicket' rhapsodizing about 'the ale, too ... barleycorn, such as would put the souls of three butchers into one weaver' and, from the Minute and Account Book, 'A wet day; only three members present: nine bottles of wine.'

John Arlott, a book-collector himself, charts the economic effects of the collectors' cult that developed after the apparent demise of the *Imbiber* in 1971 – victim of the depressions in the early 'seventies both in the wine trade and in publishing. The *Imbiber* had always been a sponsored book: wine-shippers were no longer able or at any rate ready, as in turn Gilbeys, Harveys of Bristol and then F.S. Matta had been to subsidize its publication; publishers, similarly down in the dumps, shied off producing it unsponsored.

This new *Imbiber*, I am happy to say, is not sponsored in any way: thanks to the enthusiasm of the present publisher, it stands on its own feet. So far from receiving financial favours from any purveyor of potables, the editor has paid every member of the trade whose work is printed here – every member, that is, save Philippe de Rothschild: as soon as I received his permission to reprint the nostalgic piece on his first sight of Château Mouton I realized that I knew no graceful way of offering money to a Rothschild...

John has made only one mistake. He numbers Iris Murdoch among the survivors from *Imbiber* No. 1. But no, Miss Murdoch first appeared in No. 2, and I am none the less delighted to be able to include here an extract from her Booker Prize novel *The Sea, the Sea*. Her previous contribution was *A Woman Don's Delight*: that was in 1958 – the author of *The Dons on the Dais Serene* in this 1986 Imbiber was not then born.

Another contributor to No. 2, but no longer with us, was Peter Fleming, whom I knew when I was on the staff of the *Spectator* in its convivial radical days: he contributed a weekly light essay under the pseudonym 'Strix'. I liked and admired him enormously, which I cannot say of his younger brother Ian, who, as Foreign Manager of Kemsley Newspapers, was my master when I was the *Sunday Times* correspondent in Moscow. He entertained me and my wife, to whom I had just become engaged, when I was on leave in London: this was before he had even thought of James Bond, he told me later, let alone let us hear of him, but young Liz's comment after what, I must admit, was a very good lunch, was 'that's the cruellest face I've ever seen on a man.'

There were two other brothers whom I did not know, and Peter dedicated the book of tales from which I have taken *Sherry*, reprinted here for the first time since 1942, to the youngest of the four:

To the memory of my youngest brother
MICHAEL VALENTINE FLEMING
Captain and Adjutant, 4th Bn., Oxfordshire and Buckinghamshire
Light Infantry. Mentioned in Despatches for Gallantry
Displayed on the 20th, 22nd, and 27th of May 1940
Died of his wounds while a Prisoner of War
on Oct. 1, 1940
'His complete disregard of danger and coolness
under fire were a wonderful example to all
at critical times.'

He was not yet thirty.

I think Peter would have been glad to see that dedication in print again after nearly half a century.

C.R., *Albany, London, 1986*

As a Sort of
Hors d'Oeuvre

'There is not the hundredth part of the wine consumed in this kingdom that there ought to be. Our foggy climate wants help.'

John Thorpe to Catherine Morland, Jane Austen's *Northanger Abbey*, 1818

A good, formall, precise minister in the Isle of Wight us't to say that a glasse or two of wine extraordinarie would make a man praise God with much alacritie.

Nicholas L'Estrange, *Merry Jests and Conceits*, 1630–55

Now anyone who thinks that a vivid appreciation of the exquisite flavours of wine and food implies greed, is the victim of confused thinking. Taste is one of the five senses, and the man who tells us with priggish pride that he does not care what he eats is merely boasting of his sad deficiency: he might as well be proud of being deaf or blind, or, owing to a perpetual cold in the head, of being devoid of the sense of smell. There is no reason to suppose that taste is in any way a lower sense than the other four; a fine palate is as much a gift as an eye that discerns beauty, or an ear that appreciates and enjoys subtle harmonies of sound, and we are quite right to value the pleasures that all our senses give us and educate their perceptions. The greedy man is he who habitually eats too much, knowing that he is injuring his bodily health thereby, and this is a vice to which not the *gourmet* but the *gourmand* is a slave. But Mr Harry,* though he undoubtedly was a *gourmand* also, and ate prodigious quantities of food, could not, so admirable was his digestion, and so well large masses of solid food suited him, be called greedy at all. He had a noble and healthy appetite, *le foie du charbonnier*, and as he once observed with a very proper satisfaction, 'I should like to see my stomach disagree with anything I choose to give it.'

E.F. Benson,(1867–1940),
As We Were, 1930.

She was much horrified at the way in which people in this year, 1844, gadded about. Another shocking thing was the extravagance in living: people now wanted the most elaborate dinners. 'But give me,' she said, 'a trout from my own stream, and a grouse from my own moor, and an apple tart from my own orchard, and I ask nothing more.'

E.F. Benson, *As We Were*, 1930,
quoting letter from great-aunt
to his father.

A rich soup; a small turbot; a saddle of venison; an apricot tart; this is a dinner fit for a king.

Anthelme Brillat-Savarin, (1755–1826)
La Physiologie du Goût

I look upon it, that he who does not mind his belly will hardly mind anything else.

Dr Johnson to Boswell, 5 August, 1763

* Henry Chaplin, 1840–1923, immensely rich country gentleman; won Derby of 1867, when only 27, with his 'Hermit', at 66 to one, ruining the Marquess of Hastings, who had run off with his betrothed. Cabinet Minister, created 1st Viscount Chaplin, 1916.

Postscript

How do you manage? I think you told me, at Venice, that your spirits did not keep up without a little claret. I *can* drink, and bear a good deal of wine (as you may recollect in England): but it don't exhilarate — it makes me savage and suspicious. Laudanum has a similar effect; but I can take much of *it* without any effect at all. The thing that gives me the highest spirits (it seems absurd, but true) is a dose of *salts* — I mean in the afternoon, after their effect. But one can't take *them* like champagne.

Byron: Letter to Thomas Moore (1821)

A Vintner's View

*Observations on Compleat Imbibing
from the house magazine of Berry
Brothers and Rudd (founded 1699) St. James's*

T O CONCERN oneself overmuch with the customs and traditions that have grown up around wine drinking is not too fashionable at the moment. The mood is rather to brush aside cobwebby traditions and adopt a no-nonsense attitude to the subject. It is almost *de rigueur* for a popular writer or speaker on wine to begin by declaring roundly that he proposes to cut through all the mystique and put himself in the position of the plain man in search of an honest bottle.

This down-to-earth approach is, of course, part of a general endeavour to simplify wine and persuade the British public to accept it as an everyday beverage – an endeavour that has led to such aids to the buyer as classifying all the main varieties according to a scale of dryness and sweetness. Let us make clear at once that we have a lot of sympathy with these efforts; if wine is to be established as a household drink in this country, one cannot afford to put off the potential consumer by making his first encounter with it too difficult. However, the story of wine does not end with its shelf appeal. By its nature it can never be just another commodity like a can of soup or a packet of biscuits, carrying a 'Sell by' or 'Best consumed by' date – or, if it ever were, it would no longer be wine but some processed substitute. As anyone who develops a taste for it soon discovers, wine is a mysterious product with a life and a temperament of its own and with a stubborn resistance to being reduced to simple, black-and-white terms; it needs to be approached with intelligence and treated with respect if one is to get the best out of it.

It is from this special relationship between the product of the grape and its votaries that the customs and conventions of wine drinking have evolved. And, as the merchant well knows, people continue to be very interested in the whole background to wine and anxious to find out if this or that practice connected with it is soundly based or otherwise. As Allan Sichel once pointed out, wine drinking is akin to an interest in music, poetry or painting in the way it engages and stimulates the imagination. Even the debunkers of mystique recognise this in practice, for as often as not they go on to address themselves to the very questions that have occupied wine drinkers for generations and created the cobwebby traditions – even lapsing into that much-guyed language ('winespeak', as Ronald Searle calls it) in which wine lovers try to convey to other people their elusive impressions of taste and smell.

Some wine conventions, admittedly, do not seem to have any rational explanation – or, if they do, it is lost in the mists of time. Why, for example, is it the custom to circulate the port decanter from right to left and why has it always been considered such an unforgivable social gaffe to break this rule? Various origins of the custom have been suggested, ranging from the fact that the port is then following the apparent movement of the sun to the theory that the practice is derived from Druidical funerary ceremonies. One authority on port maintained that 'Port is served from right to left because it comes from the heart' – a pleasant thought, but surely one that is applicable to every wine. However, as with many social institutions, it is a custom that people like to keep up, perhaps to give a sense of order to their lives. At the very least, it ensures that everyone at table gets his turn at the port – though maybe one need no longer take a breach of the rule quite so much to heart!

When it comes to the body of tradition on how wine should be handled and served, one is on more practical – but at the same time more subjective – ground. Is it a myth that young and middle-aged red wines benefit from being opened an hour or two beforehand so that they can 'breathe'? The view that this makes no difference at all has lately been canvassed – with the support, surprisingly, of a leading French authority, Professor Emile Peynaud, head of oenology at the University of Bordeaux, who said in a television interview that wine should be opened at the last minute if something was not to be lost from it. The argument about the serving of table wine has no bearing on how port should be treated, but here there has always been a school of thought in favour of decanting it twenty-four hours beforehand. An advocate of this practice was Lord Goddard who, when Lord Chief Justice, rightly told us: 'I am a great judge...of port'.

Our own view is that an old vintage of red table wine should be drunk as soon as possible after opening the bottle, but that younger wines do open up and 'stretch' by being allowed to come into contact with oxygen for a time. (For the same reason, we are in favour of decanting red wines even where there is no sediment to remove). Our belief seems to be borne out by those public dinners at which there can be a lapse of half-an-hour or so between the first and last glass of a particular red wine. The final glass, to our mind, usually tastes best. But those who are against letting wine 'breathe' would no doubt argue that other factors have been at work here, such as the food and the company – or, at the very least, that it is because the bottle has warmed up a bit.

This brings us to the equally debatable question of the temperature at which wine should be served. The convention is that red wine should be *chambré* by being left for a few hours in a reasonably warm room. As we have said before, we are against making too much of a fetish of temperature, otherwise one will end up hovering over the wine with a thermometer – or even adjusting the central heating! *Chambré* may be a vague concept, but it is good enough for practical purposes. However, there are people who prefer red wine, especially Beaujolais but even claret, to be cool, and we ourselves would sooner have it too cold than too warm, and certainly to having it slightly mulled by hasty heating as sometimes happens in restaurants. And while on the subject of restaurants, a custom that could happily be dropped in our opinion is serving red wine in a wicker cradle; if there is no deposit, it is unnecessary, and if there is a deposit (probably well disturbed before the bottle goes into the basket), it will still find its way into the glass.

Is it an affectation to go through the little ritual of tasting wine in a restaurant before it is served, as some of the anti-traditionalists suggest? We should have thought it was no more than a sensible precaution, because a bottle of even the most renowned and reliable

growth can occasionally be out of condition. What is slightly snobbish, perhaps, is to pretend that one can necessarily tell from one sniff and sip that the wine is all right, because sometimes – even to an experienced taster – the fault does not reveal itself until the wine has been in the glass for a minute or two.

Here we should mention, as one of the undoubted myths, the belief that mould round the cork indicates that it is rotten and that the wine will probably be 'corked'; it simply means that some liquid has got under the capsule and shows, on the contrary, that the cork is doing its job properly. By the same token, one can mention the meaningless habit of some sommeliers, perhaps trying to impress an inexperienced diner, of going through the ceremony of smelling the cork after drawing it from the bottle – meaningless because the cork would not necessarily have a nasty smell even if the wine were tainted.

One can go through most of the conventions of wine drinking and see that finally they are matters of trial and error and personal preference. The case for at least paying some heed to those conventions – for example, drinking dry wine before less dry, young before old, white before red, light before heavy – is that they represent the accumulated findings of generations of drinkers. Even so, they are not rules, but something to be verified for oneself. If someone likes sauternes with his soup or red wine with haddock, or prefers his champagne so cold that it loses its sparkle, so be it – his taste is unusual, but that is what he wants. However, there is a kind of inverse snobbery – and one that some of the no-nonsense school seem at times in danger of falling into – which implies that the only criterion is whether a wine makes an immediate appeal to the average palate. There is such a thing as education of the palate, just as there is of an ear for music or an eye for painting. The opposite of wine snobbery does not have to be a refusal to recognise that people's taste can develop and become more discriminating. The real freedom from snobbery is to approach wine without fixed ideas.

NOTE: The picture of the interior of Berry Brothers' shop is from a drypoint by Muirhead Bone, reproduced here by kind permission of Anthony Berry, for twenty years chairman of the family firm. It was Muirhead's brother, James, London Editor of the *Manchester Guardian* – the only journalist, surely, to be made a Companion of Honour – who introduced me in 1939 to Berry Brothers' shop, of which he wrote, in his *London Perambulator* (1925):

'...wine from Berry's in St. James's Street that supplied Queen Anne, and probably had had the earliest intimation of her death, a deep, low-roofed shop that not only supplied coffee, wine, and brandies to the eighteenth-century nobility of St. James's, but weighed and measured its customers, and there they are, 30,000 entries in sixteen tall folio volumes, with the two great weighing scales (one dating from the seventeenth century) and height post, still in the front shop and used by the present princes over the way*
...The cellars of Berry's were probably part of Old St. James's Palace – something like a shop!'

C.R.

---

* George V's sons

... a Consumer's ....

Keith Waterhouse

(In the course of editing
The Collected Letters of a Nobody,
Keith Waterhouse came across this *cri de coeur*
from Mr Pooter to his wine shippers)

'The Laurels'
Brickfield Terrace,
Holloway, N
April 29, 1889

To: Messrs. Jackson Frères,
    Importers of Fine Wines & Vintners' Sundrymen,
      Lower Ground Floor,
        Paxley's Varnish Warehouse,
          235, 237 & 239 Female Penitentiary Road,
        Holloway, N

My dear Sirs,
I take pen in hand as, generally speaking, a 'satisfied customer' of the excellent range of Wines and Spirits that are shipped and bottled by your good selves.

The Algerian Claret, at two and ninepence the quarter dozen, has been spoken of by connoisseurs at my table as 'cheap at the price' – a good sound Wine, free from acidity, to my untutored palate somewhat of the style of Burgundy.

Ditto the Vino Tinto, a stouter, North of Spain Wine which, being grown on Ironstone soil as I understand, has been warmly recommended by our family Doctor for my wife's blood – your Pure Port Wine having similar properties, as one may ascertain from the testimonial of Dr Esmé Shilling MD in the advertising matter at the back of *Common Diseases of Women*, it nevertheless is too full-bodied for Mrs Pooter, and gives her a splitting headache after more than one glass.

Of the White Wines, the Californian Sauterne, with which we became acquainted *via* your 'cost price sample trial' last summer, has proved a delicious dessert Wine at our supper parties, and we shall certainly have not the smallest hesitation in ordering another bottle.

As to Spirits, excepting for an unfortunate experience with so-called 'Lockanbar' whisky, to which we unwisely allowed ourselves to be introduced by a friend, I have never veered from 'Bonny Doon Five Yrs Olde.' Brandy we take 'but once in a blue moon,' Rum and the remainder never; therefore I offer no opinion. However, of your Pale Luncheon Sherry, of which we always take a convivial glass or two whilst on our annual holiday at Broadstairs, I will vouchsafe that, unlike the aforementioned watering-place, 'it has no *peer* (pier)!'

Gentlemen, it is when we turn to the celebrated 'Jackson Frerès' Medium Dry Champagne that, sorrowful although I am to say it, your Firm's motto of 'Cask-matured Quality at Moderate Prices' occasionally rings a little hollow.

Whether it has been my Wine Merchant's misfortune to have accepted delivery from your Agents of a faulty case, or whether, as he would have it, the Bouquet &c &c suffers by virtue of the bottles having to be stored upright for any length of time, since otherwise the corks sometimes fall out owing to natural shrinkage, I am not competent to say. What I *do* say - nay, I aver it! – is that we have noticed a distinct falling-off in the quality of this hitherto agreeable Wine, since first imbibing it more birthdays ago than I care to remember.

That which should, at 3/4d a bottle, be as nectar or Ambrosia, is, not to beat about that which 'no good wine needs' – i.e., the *bush* – on occasion as sour as vinegar, at the same time so lacking in effervescence that it might be one of your Still Wines at under a shilling. Indeed, a family friend, accepting a second glass of the same at my table in the course of a little celebration, went so far as to permit himself to remark, 'Pooh! This 'fizz' is as flat as the proverbial pancake!', adding that 'he should be glad when he had had enough of it'; whilst another friend, at the same table, ostentatiously scrutinised his charged glass with a facetious cry of, 'Hulloh! Cat got the bubbles?'

Now you gentlemen know your own business, and should similar complaints about this deficiency in the Champagne's 'gaseousness' have reached your ears (as I make sure they are bound to have done), then you will have weighed my Wine Merchant's theory as to the bottles losing that characteristic by being stored vertically instead of horizontally, and, should there be anything in it, will be taking steps to find the remedy – one that springs to mind is putting sealing wax around the corks to stop them falling out.

There may be, however, an alternative explanation. I am no man of science, but I would draw your attention to the strength, the lack of it, I should say – of the gas supply here in Holloway. From the over-printed address on the 'Jackson Frères' bottle label (of which more later), I gather that you have of late moved premises, just as, domestically, so have we – in our case from Shanks Place, Peckham, in yours, from Zinc Ointment Works Yard, Camberwell; in other words, we have both removed ourselves from the sphere of the South Metropolitan Gas Co., where the gas supply is of the highest quality, to that of the Imperial Gas Co., where – you must have noticed from the marked deterioration in incandescence – it is inferior. The reason, I have been told, is that the gas employed hereabouts is diluted in some way, in order to make it acceptable to the large number of balloonists in the area, who find ordinary crude gas too heavy for their purpose. I have written to the Chief Gas Examiner at Pantry Yard on the matter, but to no effect, save to lay myself open to derision. Should you, as men of commerce, however, bring to the attention of the Chief Gas Examiner the alarming fact that the local gas is so weak that it is next door to useless for the purpose of pumping bubbles into Champagne, then I believe that under the Metropolitan Gas Acts, he is obliged to take up your case.

Yet even did it possess the effervescence of Eno's Fruit Salts, I regret to say that 'Jackson Frères' suffers from one further shortcoming: it is sold too warm. We have no ice safe, such contrivances being a waste of money in my strong opinion; nor do we ever keep a bottle in the house where it could be chilling in the larder, preferring instead to send across for one as and when the requirement for the libation arises. To my mind, Champagne should be sold, ready to serve, chilled. Unfortunately, my Wine Merchant, who will be known to you as Mr Cathbone, of the Thrift Stores, St Basil's Terrace, has recently got in a large supply of cut-price lard which he keeps in his cellar, leaving no room for his Wines which are now stored in the loft, the Champagne being next to the hot-water cistern. I have made my feelings known on being fobbed off with warm Champagne, but he only says that, 'he cannot be forever moving stock around, and anyway makes so little profit out of Wines, that he is thinking of giving up the line altogether.' You would not, I am positive, wish to disclaim responsibility for the condition in which your Champagne is sold, once it has left your hands, and I wish that your Agent would have a strong word with Mr Cathbone on the subject, on his next visit.

Reverting to the 'Jackson Frères' label: as a matter of idle curiosity, do I not detect a strong resemblance between the portrait of the Brothers Jackson, and the 'before' and 'after' engravings in the advertisements for 'Lak-Goh' general debility pills; and, if this is not mere fancy, does the coincidence signify that this preparation is one of your 'sidelines,' or that the likenesses owe more to art than to life, and were simply taken willy-nilly from the printer's supply of picture-blocks? I should be most interested to know.

Despite the trifling criticisms incorporated in this letter, I remain of that legion of appreciative clientele, which Messrs Jackson Frères has served these twelve years, and hope for a speedy reply.

In haste to catch the post, I remain &c &c.,

Chas Pooter

and a Diner's-Out

'Life is Beautiful'

Edith Templeton

ERE is my recipe for finding a restaurant in a strange provincial town in Italy: think of the town as a tree, with the Corso as trunk and the inevitable Via Roma and Via Vittorio Veneto as the big branches. Turn from one side street into a yet smaller back street, branch off into an alley and walk, if possible, through a passage connecting two courtyards, and you will find the restaurants hidden like birds' nests in the thinnest boughs.

Now, on my first day in Cremona I had not yet evolved this recipe; like all good things, it took time and sore feet and unshed tears of exasperation to bring it into being. And so, finding myself for the fifth time in the cathedral square I thought I would seek out the waiter and ask his advice. But the café was empty, and the waiter was nowhere to be seen. There was a group of men standing in front of the café and they probably saw that I had reached a stage when I did not distinguish any more between dentists and antique shops and printers and specialists for chronic diseases, and they asked if they could help me.

After I had told them what I was looking for there was a moment of embarrassed silence. Then, two of the men began to talk at once: 'There are two good places in the town. The Trattoria Padovana and the Centrale.'

'Which is better?' I ask.

'Difficult to say. They are about the same.'

Names mean a lot to me. I am immediately against the Centrale. For me it has tubular lights, seats of red imitation leather, and music from a radiogram. Whereas the Padovana sounds broad beamed, old, and shadowy, restful like a brooding hen, with cream soups and wine gravies simmering on the soot-blackened range.

'Which is the way to the Padovana?' I say.

'Take the street over there, follow it till you come to an archway—' One of the men stretched out his arm and, distastefully, as though picking a worm from a box full of wriggling worms, he raised a boy by the scruff of his neck from a shrieking, scuffling entanglement of children and told him: 'You go with the lady and show her.' I was very grateful that he took my stupidity for granted, I hate it when people rely on my wits and tell me 'You can't miss it.' The Padovana lay brooding in the backyard of an untidy old house and it was most pleasant to enter the large room with its walls painted a yellowish green, against which the white-clad tables shone with a brilliance of new-laid eggs on a bed of last year's faded moss. There were no pictures, no flowers, nor any other attempt at decoration, but on the table in the centre there was a lobster, there were baskets with the yellow apples from Tyrol and bowls with lettuce leaves and bowls with those smooth, plain dark green leaves which are also a salad, and a long, narrow, smoky blue fish in jelly.

First of all I asked for red wine, and while I was waiting to be shown the menu I saw a man entering from a door at the back of the dining-room. He was tall and portly, dressed impeccably, like a man of importance, in striped trousers, a pale grey waistcoat, and a morning coat, and I watched him as he went from table to table, bowing, putting a word here and a smile there, moving on. The *padrone*.

As soon as he came up to me I recognized him. He was one of the men who had stood in front of the café on the cathedral square. But he had kept out of the talk.

'I am so pleased to see you here, madame,' he said. 'I hope you will be satisfied.'

'I am sure I will; it looks very good to me.'

He made one of those typically Italian gestures of deprecation. 'Yes, my place is supposed to be good. But you will understand, madame, that I could not tell you to come here when I saw you and you were asking for a restaurant. One must leave things to chance.'

'I would have come here if you had told me,' I say.

'I dare say you would, madame. But would you have thought of me as a man of good taste?'

We smile at each other. He bows and moves on.

I tell the waiter that I do not want *pasta*, in any shape or disguise, and he takes the blow without flinching. He offers me *coppa* instead. What is *coppa*? I want to see for myself. I see him enter a pantry and open an ice-box, one of those huge old-fashioned monuments to coolness with four separate doors and nickel hinges and panels pierced with holes arranged like stars. We had one like this at home, when I was very small, in the days when we pickled our own cucumbers and dried our own mushrooms.

He brings me on a board the lesser half of a charming looking sausage with a leathery outside and a face the size of a saucer. A minute later he serves it, carved in thin rounds, almost transparent, deep crimson, marbled with glossy white lard. It tastes rather like raw cured ham, but it has a more robust flavour. He tells me that the *coppa* is made in only two places in Italy, here in Cremona and in Parma. The Parmesan *coppa* is sweeter, the Cremonese racier, he thinks.

When he brings me the bread basket I see that the rolls are twisted and baked into adventurous shapes. They are all faintly and disarmingly zoological in their outlines. I chose one which is coiled like a snail with two horns sticking out. But I could also take one shaped like a sea cucumber or one which is a fanciful rendering of a scorpion in its death pangs.

The body of the bread is yielding like clay, and tastes of mould. The crust is thin, brittle and yellow, flaking at the merest touch. Bad dough badly baked.

The aptest thing one can say about the Cremonese rolls is that they are intriguing. This in itself is already a condemnation, because the job of the roll is to play second fiddle to other more important dishes. The roll should be to the meat what the secretary is to the executive: soothing, aiding, absorbing, and never domineering. Rolls, therefore, should look self-effacing, and when I come across rolls which rivet my attention by their very appearance I am seized at once with grave misgivings.

The rolls of Cremona should not be classed under food but under arts and decorations, and treated accordingly. The wise traveller will no more attempt to partake of them than he would break off and nibble the scroll of a façade.

*   *   *

That night, at the Padovana, I start dinner with a salad of *finocchi*. This is a round, whitish-green, fascinating vegetable, wrapped up in layers of itself which overlap like the tiles of a roof. At the top it sprouts four pale, reeded stems which bear dark green leaves, delicate, like feathers made up of needles, reminiscent of the foliage of wild asparagus. Only the round part is eaten, boiled or raw, sliced, with oil and vinegar. It has a cool, clean, nutty flavour.

After I have finished the salad, the *padrone* appears, rolling a trolley towards me. He comes, I see, I am conquered. On the trolley there is a composite dish. It is called *bollito misto*, and is the counterpart of its better-known brother the *fritto misto*. Whereas the *fritto misto* is all golden, dry, crinkled, and crisp, the *bollito* is silvery smooth and watery. Who shall say which of the two is more glorious? They must be taken according to one's mood, like the Sun and the Moon.

The *padrone* carves me a slice of boiled tongue, a sliver of boiled chicken, a chunk of boiled beef, half of a boiled calf's knuckle, and a round of a large boiled sausage. There are two sauces to go with it, the *salsa verde* and the *salsa rossa*. Intelligent as he is, he does not ask me which of the two I prefer. He knows I shall want both.

The green sauce is an enticing mixture of aromatic herbs, smoothed with oil and sharpened with vinegar. The red sauce is of an evenly thick consistency and cannot be analysed easily. Here is the recipe as told me by the *padrone*:

'Chop a shallot and fry in oil till it blushes. Add fresh tomatoes and minced carrots and butter and simmer for about twenty minutes. Add minced fresh red peppers and simmer for another ten minutes.'

For those who cannot be captivated by either of the two sauces there is another still more picturesque choice called the Mustard of Cremona.

This is a dish of fruit candied in syrup, to which a dash of pepper and mustard powder has been added. It serves as sweet spice to the mild meats and sets them on fire, in a cool and lovely way, like moonlight burning on water. The fruit is luminously transparent, like semi-precious stones. I am given a plateful. There are several cherries, unevenly rounded like antique corals; a green pear of the size of a walnut, with the black pips shining like onyx; a larger pear of the colour of rose-quartz; a green fig clouded like a flawed emerald, a curved strip of pumpkin, reddish brown and veined like chrysoprase, and the half of an apricot which could have been carved out of a topaz. They are almost too splendid to be eaten. Before starting, I ponder over their many-hued flamboyance, and come to the conclusion that the colours of the Mustard of Cremona are those found in Veronese's paintings. It is an exceedingly *raffiné* dish, a Baroque dish, sweet, full-bodied, glowing and tingling. Life is beautiful.

The Surprise of Cremona, 1954

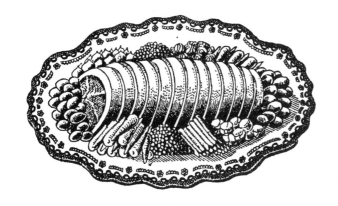

Mrs Beeton
and Mrs Dickens

Margaret Lane

I s it really more than a century that Mrs Beeton has been on the kitchen shelf? Yes, indeed, and still holding her own with a firm, ladylike touch, in spite of the great mass industry of modern cookery-book production, in spite of dieting, luncheon vouchers, frozen food, the price of beef and the disappearance of those inexhaustible Victorian servants to whom she devoted so many humane if subtly authoritarian paragraphs.

She is only barely recognizable today. Gone are those engraved coloured plates of Gothic blancmanges, the shallow dishes of roasted rabbits like beheaded babies, the towering *épergnes* dripping with muscats and smilax which would have done credit to the Veneerings' dinner-table. Instead we have colour photographs of glistening roasts (painted with glycerine in the studio, I believe) and hundreds of plain photographs of capable hands rolling pastry, larding veal, filleting fish, trussing fowls, dressing crabs, clarifying fat

33

and performing all the mysteries of the kitchen with a patient lucidity which enables even the feeblest mind to follow them.

The great improvement, indeed, of a hundred years on Mrs Beeton's original *Household Management* is in the illustrations. The early engravings are charming but inexplicit; her fish and meat look like the dolls'-house food which Tom Thumb and Hunca Munca stuffed into the kitchen range, and her puddings are one and all like Salisbury Cathedral. Whereas now, turning the pages, they make one hungry. Isabella Beeton would have approved of colour photography.

At such a size (the current volume weighs as much as a picnic ham) the great work has sacrificed the personal touch. Mrs Beeton was a young married woman, not twenty-nine when she died, who had learned housekeeping the hard way, by earnest experience, and dedicated her energies and those of her publisher husband to smoothing the path of the Victorian bride and ensuring a happy home for the Victorian husband. 'No amount of love, of beauty, or of intelligence', she wrote, 'will make home life happy without "right judgement" on the part of the housewife. A woman must rule her household, or be ruled by it; she must either hold the reins with a tight, firm hand, never parting with, but seldom using, the whip; or...the hard-working husband is placed, by his wife's indolence, under the control of his domestics, and has to depend upon their honesty and zeal alone.' Her advice is sometimes intimidating, always sound. The novice is urged to discipline, yet never to forget for a moment that she is a lady. She should glide about her house like Agnes Wickfield, with housekeeping-book and store-room keys in hand. Mrs Beeton would have had no patience with Dora Copperfield.

Life is not necessarily more complicated now than then; in some ways it is simpler. We eat less; there is not always a nurserymaid or footman to be managed, and the present-day editors refrain from giving instructions in good breeding. Yet here and there, if not in precisely her self-confident cool tone, the authentic voice of Mrs Beeton is still heard: 'Friendships should be developed gradually and not be rushed into. In many ways it is a pity the old habit of formal calls and leaving of cards is less regarded nowadays, as the greater formality of social relationships did allow a testing time for new aquaintances, which is very necessary, and which nowadays may need some tact to engineer.' It may indeed, and leisure as well as tact is noticeably scarce. It is not only our kitchens and our eating habits that have changed.

With the current edition I now possess four *Mrs Beetons*. The first, undated, was published in her lifetime, and the chapters on servants are cautionary reading. Anyone who is puzzled by the disappearance of the old-fashioned 'general' has only to turn to her Routine for the General Servant and they will clearly understand why. My next is the one my mother married with; it still has the beautiful inedible old colour plates and is a little gravy-stained; we do not use it today. The third is my own bridal volume, still much respected, as sensible and economical as ever (for it is a libel, as Nancy Spain pointed out in her biography of Mrs Beeton, to accuse her of extravagance; she never said 'First catch your hare' or dreamed of beginning a recipe with 'Take twenty eggs...'). But I have long since given up trying to fold table napkins, following its Pythagorean diagrams, into the Flat Sachet, the Mitre, the Pyramid, the Rose and Star, the Cockscomb, Fleur de Lys, the Boar's Head or the Bishop. The current edition is better printed, better illustrated and easier to read than any of its predecessors. If there is a criticism to be made, it is that it attempts too much. Nobody wants to know about the whole of life (chilblains, marriage, body lice, furnishing with antiques) from one volume.

Perhaps the most striking fact which emerges from a comparison between the early editions and the new is the change in our eating habits. Mrs Beeton's was by no means the first of the Victorian cookery-books; it was simply, being so practical and comprehensive, the most successful; and if one looks at some of the works available to her when she married, one can see at once her status as a pioneer.

I sometimes turn over the pages of a little-known volume called *What Shall We Have for Dinner?* It was published when Isabella Beeton was sixteen, written under a pseudonym, Lady Maria Clutterbuck, and was the sole literary production of Mrs Charles Dickens. (She had played the minor part of Lady Maria in an amateur theatrical production two years before.) It consists almost entirely of dinner menus, designed for two, four, six and up to twenty-four persons, offers no advice, contains only a handful of recipes, and gives a terrifying picture of Victorian hospitality. It is easier to understand Jane Carlyle's nasty remarks about the vulgarity of Dickens's dinner parties when one has studied these bills of fare. 'Such getting up of the steam is unbecoming to a literary man...The dinner was served up in the new fashion, not placed on the table at all, but handed round—only the dessert on the table and quantities of artificial flowers—but such an overloaded dessert! pyramids of figs, raisins, oranges—ach!'

When entertaining, the Victorian table was expected to groan; the status symbol was a superfluity of dishes, and the menus in Mrs Dickens's book belong to the period of Dickens's established prosperity, when he was living with his numerous family at 1 Devonshire Terrace and beginning to entertain the comparatively famous. Every course must offer at least an alternative, and nobody shrank from sickening repetition. For a little dinner for eight or ten persons Mrs Dickens recommends three soups, four fish dishes, eleven separate dishes of meat and game, three different cream puddings and a savoury. When lobsters are in season she offers boiled salmon with lobster sauce *and* filleted lobster for the first course, lobster cutlets in the second, and, after the usual three puddings and a savoury, lobster salad. Mrs Beeton, a few years later, did much to break down the habits of ostentation at the table, and of overeating. She was an enemy to waste, doing much to pave the way for reasonable catering.

Economies of this sort, however, did not appeal to Dickens, who had known too well what it was to be hungry as a boy, and who seems ever after to have remained strongly emotional in his attitude to food. This, of course, is common to us all; what is unusual and significant in Dickens is the extent to which he uses it in his novels as a means of displaying character or evoking emotion. At Mr Dombey's Christmas party, on a bitter cold day, there is cold veal, cold calf's head, cold fowls, ham, patties, salad and lobster. The wine is so cold that it 'forces a little scream from Miss Tox', and through all this shuddering and unfestive meal 'Mr Dombey alone remained unmoved'. The coy warmth, on the other hand, with which Dickens describes Ruth Pinch's rolling-out of a suet crust makes even a beefsteak pudding seem erotic. Food and drink are so pre-eminently his symbols of cheer and security that in the early novels they are inclined to run away with him. (In *Pickwick Papers* there are twenty-five breakfasts, thirty-two dinners, ten luncheons, ten teas and eight suppers, while drink is mentioned 249 times.) Nevertheless Dickens himself was a fairly abstemious man, and if his wife's menus make a contradictory impression, that is because they aim at the mid-Victorian ideal, to which he whole-heartedly subscribed, of full feeding as the soul of hospitality.

The disgrace of the potato is a modern phenomenon, unthought of a hundred years ago, when nearly everyone, man, wife and maiden aunt, was stout at forty. In nearly all of Mrs Dickens's family menus potatoes appear in at least two distinct guises, usually 'mashed and brown'—a practice I have encountered only once in my life, when I dined years ago with a Conservative M.P. in his chambers in the Temple. He had an aged cook who had waited on single gentlemen all her life, and the potatoes came up in the grand Victorian mode, mashed and roast, in covered silver dishes.

Suet and starch are two other modern casualties, figuring largely in Mrs Beeton's early work, as in Mrs Dickens's. (The two dishes of potatoes accompanying the Dickens roast will be followed by suet roll, with macaroni as a savoury.) Dickens himself appears not to have had a particularly sweet tooth, or to have satisfied it chiefly with 'milk punch' and other hot, spiced and sweetened drinks, of which many recipes have survived from the days of Georgina Hogarth's efficient housekeeping. (A raw egg beaten up in a glass of sherry or champagne was the pick-me-up on which he relied during his reading tours.) Mrs Dickens's menus are singularly repetitive in their puddings, and more meals than one would have thought possible end with bloaters. A Yarmouth bloater, like toasted cheese, was a favourite savoury at Devonshire Terrace, but to find it recommended again and again for a 'dinner for four or five people', at the end of a substantial meal and following say, apple fritters or a boiled batter pudding, suggests almost an obsession.

The emphasis on rich and starchy dishes, as well as the monotony of Mrs Dickens's collection, makes one wonder whether Dickens's growing distaste for his marriage, which culminated in the famous breach and in prolonged unhappiness for both parties, may not have been—at least partly—due to the fact that while still young she became mountainously fat. Professor A.A. Adrian, in his biography of Catherine Dickens's sister, Georgina Hogarth, scotched the persistent rumour that the trouble was due to her having, like some other Victorian ladies, taken secretly to drink. This, it seems, was not so, but a fondness for some of her own recipes alone would account for the monstrous alteration in her appearance by the end of the Devonshire Terrace period. Her Italian Cream, to take a recurring example, begins—'Whip together for nearly an hour a quart of very thick scalded cream, a quart of raw cream...with ten ounces of white powdered sugar, then add half-a-pint of sweet wine and continue to whisk until it is quite solid...'

Poor lady, she would have done better to follow the advice of Mrs Beeton, but alas, she was born too soon; the cookery-books of her time thought nothing of gallons of cream and quantities of beaten yolks and powdered sugar, accepting these things in the lavish dairy-and-stillroom tradition of the eighteenth century. Her late husband, she wrote in her Preface, addressing her readers in the character of Sir Jonas Clutterbuck's widow, had been a man of very good appetite and excellent digestion, 'and I am consoled in believing that my attention to the requirements of his appetite secured me the possession of his esteem until the last'. There is a sad irony, as one turns the page of this muddled, inept and unhelpful little book, in calculating the short space of time between its appearance and the harsh withdrawal of Dickens' esteem for ever. A few years after the book's appearance the door was walled up between his room and hers, and the following year saw the separation agreement. The 'matutinal meal' was no longer 'a time to dread, only exceeded in its terrors by the more awful hour of dinner'. Dickens was remote and indifferent at Gad's Hill, and there was no longer anyone but herself to cater for.

Purely for Pleasure, 1966

good and made by somebody else is pretty intolerable at any time. It seems to me an inconvenient and much overrated drink, but this I will admit to be a matter of personal taste. (Whereas other views which I hold on the subject of food approximate to absolute truths.) I do not normally eat at breakfast time since even half a slice of buttered toast can induce an inconvenient degree of hunger, and eating too much breakfast is a thoroughly bad start to the day. I am however not at all averse to elevenses which can come in great variety. There are, as indicated above, moments for oranges. There are also moments for chilled port and plum cake.

The orange feast did not dim my appetite for lunch, which consisted of fish cakes with hot Indian pickle and a salad of grated carrot, radishes, watercress and bean shoots. (I went through a period of grated carrot with everything, but recovered.) Then cherry cake with ice cream. I had mixed feelings about ice cream until I realized that it must always be eaten with a cake or tart, never with fruit alone. By itself it is of course pointless, even if stuffed with nuts or other rubbish. And by 'ice cream' I mean the creamy vanilla sort. 'Flavoured' ice cream is as repugnant to the purist as 'flavoured' yoghurt. Nor have I ever been able to see the *raison d'être* of the so-called 'water ice', which transforms itself offensively on the tongue from a searing lump of hard frozen material into a mouthful of equally tasteless water. I am grieved that my lack of a refrigerator involves me in a marginal waste of food. My refrigeratorless mother never wasted a crumb. Everything not consumed lived to fight another day. How we loved her bread puddings!

It is after lunch and I shall now describe the house. For lunch, I may say, I ate and greatly enjoyed the following: anchovy paste on hot buttered toast, then baked beans and kidney beans with chopped celery, tomatoes, lemon juice and olive oil. (Really good olive oil is essential, the kind with a taste, I have brought a supply from London.) Green peppers would have been a happy addition only the village shop (about two miles pleasant walk) could not provide them. (No one delivers to far-off Shruff End, so I fetch everything, including milk, from the village.) Then bananas and cream with white sugar. (Bananas should be cut, *never* mashed, and the cream should be thin.) Then hard water biscuits with New Zealand butter and Wensleydale cheese. Of course I never touch foreign cheeses. Our cheeses are the best in the world. With this feast I drank most of a bottle of Muscadet out of my modest 'cellar'. I ate and drank slowly as one should (cook fast, eat slowly) and without distractions such as (thank heavens) conversation or reading. Indeed eating is so pleasant one should even try to suppress thought. Of course reading and thinking are important but, my God, food is important too. How fortunate we are to be food-consuming animals. Every meal should be a treat and one ought to bless every day which brings with it a good digestion and the precious gift of hunger.

I wonder if I shall ever write my *Charles Arrowby Four Minute Cookbook*? The 'four minutes' of course refer to the active time of preparation, and do not include unsupervised cooking time. I have looked at several so-called 'short order' cookery books, but these works tend to deceive, their 'fifteen minutes' really in practice means thirty, and they contain instructions such as 'make a light batter'. The sturdy honest persons to whom my book would be addressed would not necessarily be able to make a light batter or even to know what it was. But they would be hedonists. In food and drink, as in many (not all) other matters, simple joys are best, as any intelligent self-lover knows. Sidney Ashe once offered to initiate me into the pleasures of vintage wine. I refused with scorn. Sidney hates ordinary wine and is unhappy unless he is drinking some expensive stuff with a date on it. Why wantonly destroy one's palate for cheap wine? (And by that I do not of course mean the brew that tastes of bananas.) One of the secrets of a happy life is continuous small treats, and if some of these can be inexpensive and quickly procured so much the better. Life in the theatre often precluded serious meals and I have not always in the past been able to eat slowly, but I have certainly learnt how to cook quickly. Of course my methods (especially a liberal use of the tin opener) may scandalize fools, and the various people (mainly the girls: Jeanne, Doris, Rosemary, Lizzie) who urged me to publish my recipes did so with an air of amused condescension. Your name will sell the book, they tactlessly insisted. 'Charles's meals are just picnics', Rita Gibbons once remarked. Yes, good, even great, picnics. And let me say here that *of course* my guests *always* sit squarely at tables, never balance plates on their knees, and *always* have proper table napkins, *never* paper ones.

Food is a profound subject and one, incidentally, about which no writer lies. I wonder whence I derived my felicitous gastronomic intelligence? A thrifty childhood gave me a horror of wasted food. I thoroughly enjoyed the modest fare we had at home. My mother was a 'good plain cook', but she lacked the inspired simplicity which is for me the essence of good eating. I think my illumination came, like that of Saint Augustine, from a disgust with excesses. When I was a young director I was idiotic and conventional enough to think that I had to entertain people at well-known restaurants. It gradually became clear to me that guzzling large quantities of expensive, pretentious, often mediocre food in public places was not only immoral, unhealthy and unaesthetic, but also unpleasurable. Later my guests were offered simple joys *chez moi*. What is more delicious than fresh hot buttered toast, with or without the addition of bloater paste? Or plain boiled onions with a little cold corned beef if desired? And well-made porridge with brown sugar and cream is a dish fit for a king. Even then some people, so sadly corrupt was their taste, took my intelligent hedonism for an affected eccentricity, a mere gimmick. (*Wind in the Willows* food a journalist called it.) And some were actually offended.

However, it may be that what really made me see through the false mythology of *haute cuisine* was not so much restaurants as dinner parties. I have long, and usually vainly, tried to persuade my friends not to cook grandly. The waste of time alone is an absurdity; though I suppose it is true that some unfortunate women have nothing to do but cook. There is also the illusion that very elaborate cooking is more 'creative' than simple cooking. Of course (let me make it clear) I am not a barbarian. French country food, such as one can still occasionally find in that blessed land, is very good; but its goodness belongs to a tradition and an instinct which cannot be aped. The pretentious English hostess not only mistakes elaboration and ritual for virtue; she is also very often exercising her deluded art for the benefit of those who, though they would certainly not admit it, do not really enjoy food at all. Most of my friends in the theatre were usually so sozzled when they came to eat a serious meal that they had no appetite and in any case scarcely knew what was set before them. Why spend nearly all day preparing food for people who eat it (or rather toy with it and leave it) in this condition? A serious eater is a moderate drinker. Food is also spoilt at dinner parties by enforced conversation. One's best hope is to get into one of those 'holes' where one's two neighbours are eagerly engaged elsewhere, so that one can concentrate upon one's plate. No, I am no friend of these 'formal' scenes which often have more to do with vanity and prestige and a mistaken sense of social 'propriety' than with the true instincts of hospitality. *Haute cuisine* even inhibits hospitality, since those who cannot or will not practise it hesitate to invite its devotees for fear of seeming rude or a failure. Food is best eaten among friends who are unmoved by such 'social considerations', or of course best of all alone. I hate the falsity of 'grand' dinner parties where, amid much kissing, there is the appearance of intimacy where there is really none.

After this tirade it looks as if the description of the house will have to wait until another day. I might add here that (as will already be evident) I am not a vegetarian. In fact I eat very little meat, and hold in horror the 'steak house carnivore'. But there are certain items (such as anchovy paste, liver, sausages, fish) which hold as it were strategic positions in my diet, and which I should be sorry to do without; here hedonism triumphs over a peevish baffled moral sense. Perhaps I ought to give up eating meat, but by now, when the argument has gone on so long, I doubt if I ever will.

The narrator in *The Sea, the Sea*, 1978

Bingo for Bifteck: Lotto in the Lot

Ruth Silvestre

E arrive early because we were warned again only that morning. '*Il faut y aller de bonne heure pour trouver une chaise,*' she had shouted, and everyone in the village shop had agreed, eyes bright in anticipation of the evening's excitement.

It is due to begin at nine, this Lotto, as bingo is called in France. Half an hour later, as the outdoor faces that usually smile at us from a tractor or from between a row of vines are still crowding into the room we realise that the starting time will all depend on just how long each takes to greet each other.

'*Bonsoir.*' '*Bonsoir.*'

'*Ça va?*' '*Ça va.*'

Kiss, kiss and yet another for luck.

'How warm it is for the time of the year.'

'Yes. And the ground is so wet. *Pardis!*'

With smiles and the Gallic shrugs they pass on to the next neighbour.

We buy our cards for the evening at 25F for four. They are dog-eared and judging by the rubber stamp in one corner have been borrowed from the next commune. Along the length of the tables, like harvest festival, are small heaps of maize with which to cover the numbers as they are called out. The caller blows into the microphone. Café owner and shopkeeper, tender of vines and cattle, strawberries and petrol pumps, there seems no end to his expertise. His mischievous grandson eyes the large drum of numbered plastic balls and is swiftly removed.

'*Alors ... Mesdames. Messieurs. Il faut commencer.*'

As they settle down, the prizes for the first game of the evening are announced.

'*Pour la première ligne...un filet garni. Pour deux lignes...un poulet. Une bouteille de bon vin. La carte complète...un jambon.*' The hall is hushed.

After the first few games are completed and we watch the delighted winners stow away *rôtis* of veal and pork, and jars of *confit de canard* or prunes in eau-de-vie – all produced locally – we begin to understand just why bingo in rural France is an event not to be missed. When all the prizes are edible it is a serious affair.

Our immediate neighbours keep an eye on our cards as well as their own, and we are slightly ashamed to find ourselves surreptitiously checking each other in English – especially the numbers over 60. We console ourselves with the fact that the caller insists on shouting the occasional number in 'Occitan' or 'patois,' to cries of protest from the youngsters but to the obvious delight of the older generation.

At 10.30 it is time for the *entr'acte*. In this region of the *vieux* Cahors, where the arrival of the Beaujolais creates hardly a ripple, they all appear on this occasion to confine themselves to 'Orangina' or 'le Schweppes'; but how they eat! Huge dishes of *beignets* and piles of rolled up *crêpes* appear and then vanish; the children play beneath the tunnels of the long tables and the whole room reverberates with happy voices.

'*Alors*'...Eyes down again. The prizes vary. Two pheasants, a turkey, and for the whole card, a *tourtière*. Proud speciality of the region, this spectacular apple pie is presented for admiration. On a thin pastry base, the interior is a soft melange of sweetened apple purée and rum or *eau-de-vie de prune*. It is crowned with tissue-thin curls of pastry which has taken hours of stretching on a farmhouse kitchen table before being lovingly arranged in this intricate sculpture. People have given generously as all the proceeds are to help the village school – one *assistante* and fourteen pupils.

There is a new excitement when a surprise lot is announced. It is revealed at last to be a pair of live wild ducks. With wings flapping they are presented to a beaming farmer's wife who stands up to display with pride the male with his glistening green head and his drab consort.

'*Faites libre! Faites libre!*' chants the crowd banging the tables. Not a chance. She knows their precise value for breeding and returning them gently to their box she soothes the ruffled feathers with a practised hand as she grins at her husband. What fun it all is!

At long last, the final game and the prize for which we have all been waiting.

'*Une cuisse de boeuf!*' yells the caller, somewhat husky now. Eighteen kilos of prime beef and the collective palate of the room drools at the thought. Eighteen kilos of *le bifsteak*, with garlic of course — perhaps grilled with shallots and parsley. Perhaps even *en daube* with *cèpes*, those thick white-fleshed toadstools that arrive as though by magic after the first September rainfall and begin days of frenzied searching in the steaming woods.

Passionate discussions of favourite recipes explode about the room while the weary caller pleads for attention. It has already gone midnight and many of the children are asleep, tousled heads among the doughnut crumbs. At last there is a silence and the game begins.

The rolling accent of the Southwest is loud and strong.

'*Quatre-vingt trois. Cinquante et un.*'

The tension mounts as we look at each other's cards. Only one more needed there, and over there too.

'*Trente-sept. Quatorze.*' he intones solemnly.

Sturdy hands are poised over the cards, the grain of maize squeezed between finger and thumb.

'*Quatre-vingt dix-sept.*'

A great shout goes up followed by the sighs and groans of the losers, and a young father of five is on his feet flushed with triumph. A woman tells us that last year two old ladies won a pig between them and argued for a week over who should keep it. I suppose they might just come if the prizes were mere money but it wouldn't be half as much fun. The winners pack their prizes carefully into cartons and the children are throwing handfuls of maize at each other as we all reel out into the dark and starry night.

Guardian, 2 August 1985

Investing in Futures:
a Story

Kingsley Amis

T HERE'S no risk involved and no one else I can send,' the Director said imploringly. 'Please help me, you four— we've been through a lot together, after all. I just have to know the answer about those damned vines. And you appreciate why.'

Our association had started back in the old days of the first temporal probes. Then, under a still-secret programme, the government had used our Unit to explore the nearer future and find answers to some of its more awkward problems. And we of the Unit, being all of us rather interested in the fortunes of our own chosen kind of alcoholic drink, had privately used those chances to explore the future of vintage port (the Director's obsession), my own humble draught beer, and so on with the rest of the team.

All that was over. The probes had long been stopped as uneconomic. The Unit was disbanded and the Director had for years been, officially, sadly, the ex-Director. But he had sounded quite as excited and secretive as his old self when, two days previously, he had telephoned me and asked me to get the others together at an obscure address in Soho. The four of us had turned up on the dot, all agog.

He had begun no less mysteriously by running over the known and abominated career of phylloxera XO, the deadly sub-species of vine-aphid first seen in the Bordeaux vineyards in 1984, classified and named in California three years later, rampaging everywhere by the end of the '80s and now, in 1993, the apparently invincible curse that had reduced world wine-production to 59% of 1986 levels. He continued with fresh data: using revolutionary forced-growth techniques, French agricultural scientists had succeeded in developing five new strains of vine, which early tests had shown to be resistant to all forms of phylloxera including the XO. But early tests were early tests: it would take ten years of growth in the soil, of successive harvests, of standing up to the assaults of the deadly little insects before any of the new strains could be pronounced proof against them and systematic replanting begun. Five special areas in Burgundy were ready for the ten-year trials. 'And that,' the Director had said with relish, 'is where we come in. Literally. Or to be even more precise, it's where you come in, Simpson.'

At that old Simpson, our traveller on previous time-trips, just gaped.

'Yes. You're off to the year 2003 as soon as we can arrange it. You'll bring back reports on all five of the experimental vineyards. Cuttings too if possible.'

'Against Temporal Regs, sir,' I objected. 'Inter-sectoral transfers are out.'

'I'm sorry, Baker, we'll have to overlook that. This whole thing is—well, not very official anyway, or even legal. But just consider. Frankly, I'm not a rich man. I doubt whether any of you are either— one doesn't get rich in this business. But anyone who knows the result of those long-term trials now, in 1993, is going to know something very valuable. Do you—if I may so express myself—read me?'

There was a new stir of interest. 'But how would anyone get there, sir?' I demurred. 'All the hardware was broken up ages ago.'

'That's where you're wrong. At least not all of it has proved impossible to reassemble. With a little goodwill. If all goes well we could share the cost, eh?'

'I'm ten years out of touch, sir.' This was Rabaiotti, my senior assistant.

'We're all getting on a bit, sir,' said Schneider, our former MO.

Which was when the director came out with the appeal I quoted earlier, and after that it was just a question of detail. When, the following week, we assembled in a sort of dungeon off Whitehall we found waiting for us the good old modified TALISKER (Temporal Accelerator with Latent-Indeterminacy Suppressor and Kinetic-Energy Recompensator) that had served us so well in the past – or should I say, in bygone futures? Rabaiotti fed the power, took a long look, ran his hands over the relay banks, nodded slowly at me and started punching co-ordinates. Schneider was passing his hand-scanner over Simpson. The Director called me over to meet a tall swarthy man whom he introduced as a friend of his, a Dr Hanif Khan.

I didn't know why, but I immediately felt there was something odd about Dr Khan, not suspect exactly, just odd, something too that was unknown to the Director. Before speaking Khan produced what looked like a small old-fashioned television set with attachments but which I recognised as one of the new boson microscopes.

'I'm a botanist specialising in vines,' Khan said. His manner was disarming enough. 'Used to be quite a tough job, you know. Not any more, thanks to this jigger. Quite frightening, what it can see. In fact nobody seems quite sure what it can't see. Anyway, one thing it will certainly be able to see is whatever we may want to know about what your chap brings back from, er, over the way. No problem.'

I nodded appreciatively.

'Well, Hanif,' the Director said, 'would you like to run your eye over our baby here? If you have any questions I'll no doubt prove incompetent to answer them.'

True enough. I made to go along but Khan politely held up his hand.

'You've plenty to see to, Dr Baker. I mustn't interfere with any of that.'

So I let them get on with it while I checked and rechecked the settings with Rabaiotti, sat Simpson on the stool and pressed the SEND/RETURN strap, a feature of the TALISKER that caused him to vanish and reappear in no time at all, though subjectively he had spent over four hours away. There was some dirt on his face and rather more on his clothes; otherwise he seemed none the worse. Schneider forbade contact until he had scanned him out, micro-scoured him and handed him a large Scotch and water. Then we crowded round and listened to his story.

The date keyed into the TALISKER was 15 July 2003, selected on the reasoning that after celebrating Bastille Day the day before many Frenchmen would be in a state of reduced curiosity and vigilance when Simpson turned up in their midst. As it happened nobody saw him arrive in a secluded hollow in the hills above Beaune. At once aware of the great surrounding silence, he checked his position and surveyed his route.

It was 4 pm and the sun was shining. The special vineyards lay grouped round a central research station seven kilometres to the south-west. He had plenty of time to make his way to that station and, in the character of a visiting oenologist from New South Wales, fix himself a brief tour of the vineyards. If unable to secure cuttings or in any other difficulty he was to conceal himself and operate after dark.

His journey would be made on foot, Temporal Regulations strongly disfavoured the use of futural transport and, after an encounter with a subway escalator in 2062, he had been happy to abide by them. With a last check of map and compass (stereomap and lumen-compass, naturally) he set off in good spirits down the grassy slopes. Once or twice he took a deep breath. The air was strikingly pure, even for such a very remote spot as this appeared, though the bird population was plentiful and busy enough.

Simpson was a claret man and had often visited the Bordeaux villages and vineyards, and if he had known those of Burgundy even one-quarter as well he might have started to ask himself questions sooner than he did. As it was he went happily on until a glance at the map showed he should be near the main Beaune-Pommard road—no, wait: should have crossed it a hundred metres back. There was no such road on the ground, no road at all anywhere that he could see, though he had passed close to more than one earth track. What was to be seen of the work of man? From higher up he had spotted a couple of churches, a large house with towers at each end, the roofs of a small village, a windmill. From here a rutted path led past a crude wooden hut and out of sight. Poor crops of some unfamiliar

cereal—millet, perhaps, or rye—covered part of the hillside. Nothing else.

He had decided that he must have crossed that road after all, that the mud-slide he remembered picking his way over had surely buried a long section of it, when he heard voices approaching round the bend of the path he was standing on. Without hesitation he ran for the shelter of a low bank topped with bushes and peered out from there. He could not have said what had induced him to hide.

In a moment a farm-cart of sorts drawn by a skinny horse rattled and jolted into view. A lank-haired fellow of about thirty held the reins and plied a whip, an older man sat beside him, another man and a woman lolled in the body of the cart among a load of swedes or other root-crop. The four were calling out roughly to one another in what Simpson, with his goodish but limited French, identified as an uncouth local dialect. All were deeply tanned, none wore anything much better than rags, and a strong animal odour drifted across as they went by. The impression they gave of brutal debasement was overpowering.

Before they were out of sight a dreadful suspicion from the back of Simpson's mind had hardened into certainty. Twice in 1991 the world had come near to war, first over the Khvoy incident, then again during the siege of Durban. The third crisis must have come and this time not gone away. What he had just been looking at was a group of the survivors, the pitiful remnants of humanity after the great catastrophe. But was such thoroughgoing degeneration possible in ten years or less? Had the TALISKER taken him further into the future than intended? Firmly he thrust away such futile guessing-games and concentrated his mind first on the Temporal Regulation requiring every mission to be carried out to the full extent possible, and then on what could still be in it for him. After a short rest and ten mg of paracynomyl he was on his way to the research station, or whatever might remain of it.

Nothing remained of it—at least, nothing he could discern under the thicket of brambles and briers that covered the site—but there were remnants of the surrounding vineyards, if the sickly, stunted plants now growing there were truly such. But part of his task was to take cuttings and he proceeded to do so. Absorbed in this, he failed to heed the approach of the watchman. There was a struggle; he took a blow on the head and perhaps lost consciousness for a time. Anyhow he remembered nothing clearly till he was sitting on

the bare stone floor of a large antiquated kitchen with an upper servant of some kind, as it might have been a steward, demanding to
know who he was. (These and some later inferences were reached by
Simpson or one or other of his audience as he told his tale.)

As soon as the steward saw Simpson's credentials his manner
changed from irate suspicion to caution if not respect. He bustled
off, returning with a man in his fifties who could be positively identified from his dress and tonsure as an ecclesiastic, a monk. But any
hopes Simpson might have had of understanding treatment from a
man of learning were soon dashed. The cleric studied the typewrit-
ten documents briefly and uneasily, darting similar glances at
Simpson and his no doubt strange-seeming get-up. Finally he thrust
the papers back at him, snapped an order to the steward in his odd
sibilant patois and unceremoniously withdrew.

It was not much, but it was toleration. Simpson was placed near
one end of a long oak table, brought water in response to his mim-
ings and left free to take stock of his surroundings. Light came from
a few stubby candles and a vast open fire above which joints of meat
sizzled. The air was hot, smoky and heavy with cooking and other
smells. Hams and other preserved eatables hung from the ceiling.
There was a great coming and going of attendants with serving-
dishes and general carry-on until the main business of getting the
meal up to the monks' dining-hall was accomplished. At this stage
of the game the steward, now seen as a likeable character in a fine
embroidered jacket, no doubt a relic of happier times, settled himself next to Simpson and genially indicated that he should help himself to food and drink.

There was no shortage of either: mutton, cold fowl, sausage,
coarse bread, butter, cheese, fresh berries, beer, red wine, all set out
at once and indiscriminately. As he had begun to guess with the
songbirds, Simpson saw while he piled his plate that whatever had
assailed humanity had not affected other forms of life.

Or had it? He was hungry and the ambient smells were so heavy
that his jaws had closed on a lump of mutton before he was aware
that it was putrid, turning rotten. The steward saw his distress, nodded cheerfully and passed him a crock of salt. Wary of giving
offence, Simpson managed a couple of nauseating mouthfuls. The
fowl was a little better, if only because the gamey reek seemed less
incongruous; the seasoning of the sausage burnt his tongue. The
fruit was sour, the cheese quite frightening. Pushing aside the rancid

butter he tried the bread, but it was full of gritty residues. The watery beer at least offset some of the salt, until after a few swallows its mawkish flavour became too much. It was out of pure sense of mission that he accepted a pot of wine.

No use trying for the nose in this place. He took a sip, then more. Often since that evening in the bowels of Whitehall Simpson has tried to describe that wine of which perhaps 50 ml passed down his throat. It was not exactly that it was unlike any other wine he had ever tasted, nor yet that it was finer, nobler: it was greater in sheer size. If a Château Haut Brion at the top of its form could be compared with a fragrance of Cathay, then what he drank now was all the riches of the East. He lowered the cup and gazed at the steward, who took it from him with a grimace of apology and stirred into it watered honey and a spoonful of some herbal infusion. With admirable fortitude he sampled the result, and had some difficulty describing that too, though some of the phrases he used were most evocative.

Wide-eyed, hand on stomach, Simpson lurched from the kitchen to the accompaniment of good-natured jeers and shouts of encouragement. But he was not really ill. Once in the open he completed the circuit in the bracelet on his wrist and the TALISKER had him safe and sound.

Dr Khan was twitching with excitement. He shook Simpson's hand a dozen times, almost snatched the vine cuttings from him and placed them in the field of his microscope. Its screen remained blank for nearly a minute while we all stared at it as if hypnotised. Then several rows of symbols flashed up together. Khan pressed buttons once, twice, got new answers and gave a great sigh. With a flourish he cleared the machine and, very much master of ceremonies, turned and faced his audience.

'What Dr Simpson has brought us,' Khan began, 'is something altogether more interesting and shall I say more *valuable* than the result of any immunological experiment. We have in our possession not the latest of vines but the first, not a mutation but the rootstock, the *Urrebe*. As confirmed just now by archaeobotanical comparison, it is a living specimen of the extinct primeval wine-grape bearer, *vitis vinifera pristina*, of which more in a moment. First I have some explaining and apologising to do, and first of all to you, sir.'

Here he bowed to the Director, who sent the rest of us a nervous smile.

'While you were most lucidly explaining to me the tuning of your temporal transmitter I was impertinent enough to distract your attention and change the setting in a most radical way. Yes, as he must already have begun to suspect, Dr Simpson has visited not the future but the past, the late 14th century I should judge—I wasn't too sure of the calibration. Dr Simpson, I do beg your pardon for my reckless and high-handed—'

The Director had turned the colour of a fine Tavel rosé and was speechless, but Simpson had opened a transparent packet and taken out a small metal object which he passed up to Khan. 'I didn't only collect vines back there. That's the salt-spoon I was handed by the steward—or perhaps I should say the seneschal.'

Khan reactivated his appliance, inserted the spoon and lowered a bar. 'This may take a little longer. Er, as I say, I'm afraid I was really most rash.'

'It was worth it,' Simpson said. 'One thing—I don't understand why that monk reacted as he did. I see now he couldn't have read a word of my papers, but it was as if he was afraid of them.'

Rabaiotti grinned. 'Of course he was afraid of them. Documents in an unknown language produced by an unknown method? Think yourself lucky not to have been dragged out and burnt on the spot.'

'If it had been anywhere else but a monastery ...'

'Everything one had ever thought about the Middle Ages, eh? Notably the horrid—'

A bleeper started up on the microscope and the screen illuminated itself. 'Compounded—in other words put together, made—AD 1325 plus or minus five' Khan announced. 'Apparent age 19 plus or minus one. A little earlier than I estimated.'

'Nice to think it might have been 1346,' I said. 'Edward III and the Black Prince moving in to clobber the Frogs at Crécy. What if they'd been on the look-out for English spies?'

'Burgundy wasn't part of France then,' Schneider put in.

'Could we have some order, gentlemen?' the Director called. 'I'd like to hear more from Dr Khan about just how valuable this thing is.'

'Thank you, sir. Our discovery, our prize is reproducible and fructifiable or will be within a short time. Soon we shall be enjoying the wine that Dr Simpson's hosts found too feeble to drink unadulterated. And marketing the living vines that produce it.'

'Splendid, but for how long?' Rabaiotti asked. 'Why should we imagine that this *vitis pristina* will be any more proof against phyl-loxera than the vines we know?'

'Because of its natural defences,' Khan said earnestly. 'Those defences that human beings have almost as if deliberately destroyed with the very chemicals meant to improve them. Once, *phylloxera vastatrix* was an almost harmless little beast—almost, not quite. So he had to be sprayed out of existence, and indeed he was ousted tem-porarily, only to return with greater strength against a weakened prey. And the next time was worse.

'The dates will show you. First organised spraying of French vines, 1803, under Chaptal, Napoleon's minister of the interior. First severe phylloxera damage, 1811–12. First toxic smoke attempts, 1859. New phylloxera penetration into Loire vineyards, 1865. And so on. That was my first clue. The medicine on which the disease flourished was progressively undermining the patient. And incidentally it seems the price the vines paid for sheer survival was loss of quality in the product. As always. There's not much meat on a mountain goat.

'So ... soon, very soon, we here will collectively launch what will be nothing less than the wine of the century—the 21st century, that is, by courtesy of the 14th!'

It was quite soon, in 1997 to be exact, and I was there when the corks were pulled at the first tasting, and by universal consent the wine was absolutely horrible. It hadn't travelled, so to speak. But by then we, the six of us, had all cleaned up.

Rumpole and the Blind Tasting: a Story

John Mortimer

UMPOLE! How could you possibly drink that stuff?'

'Perfectly easy, Erskine-Brown. Raise the glass to the lips, incline the head slightly backwards and let the liquid flow gently past the tonsils. I admit I've had a good deal of practice, but even you may come to it in time.'

I was sitting in Pommeroy's Wine Bar licking some grievous wounds inflicted on me by His Honour Judge Roger Bullingham (known to me as the Mad Bull) whose brutal and biased summing up had led to my having to say goodbye to a client named Harry 'Snakelegs' Johnson for a period of anything up to four years. I would miss 'Snakey': he and I had been through some fine legal battles together.

'Of course you can drink it, Rumpole. Presumably you could drink methylated spirits shaken up with a little ice and a dash of angostura bitters.' Erskine-Brown's dialogue was showing some unaccustomed vivacity. 'The point is, why on earth should you want to?'

'Forgetfulness, Erskine-Brown. The consignment of the way the Mad Bull interrupted my cross-examination to the Lethe of forgotten things. And intoxication. The reason for drinking Château Fleet Street,' and I drained the large claret Jack Pommeroy had obligingly put on my slate until the next legal-aid cheque came in, 'the aim, not to put too fine a point on it, is to get pissed.'

'The purpose of drinking wine is not intoxication, Rumpole.' Erskine-Brown looked as pained as a prelate who is told that his congregation only came to church because of the central heating. 'The point of drinking wine is to get in touch with one of the major influences of western civilization, to taste sunlight trapped in a

57

bottle, and to remember some stony slope in Tuscany or a village by the Gironde.'

I thought with a momentary distaste of the bit of barren soil, no doubt placed between the cowshed and the pissoir, where the Château Pommeroy grape struggles for existence. And then Erskine-Brown, long time member of our chambers in Equity Court, opera-lover, wine connoisseur, half-hearted prosecutor and inept defender, spouse and helpmeet to Miss Phillida Trant, the Portia of our chambers who had taken silk, leaving poor old Claude Erskine-Brown, ten years older than she, a humble junior, went considerably too far.

'You see, Rumpole,' he said, 'it's the terrible nose.'

Now I make no particular claim for my nose and I am far from suggesting that it's a thing of beauty and a joy forever. When I was in my perambulator it may, for all I can remember, have had a sort of tip-tilted and impertinent charm. In my youth it was no doubt pinkish and healthy looking. In my early days at the bar it had a sharp and inquisitive quality that made prosecution witnesses feel they could keep no secrets from it. Today it is perhaps past its prime; it has spread somewhat; it has, in part at least, gone mauve; it is, after all, a nose that has seen a considerable quantity of life. But man and boy it has served me well and I had no intention of having my appearance insulted by Claude Erskine-Brown, barrister-at-law, who looks, in certain unfavourable lights, like an abbess with a bad period.

'We may disagree about the Château Thames-Embankment,' I told him, 'but that's no reason why you should descend to personal abuse.'

'No, I don't mean *your* nose, Rumpole. I mean the *wine*'s nose.'

I looked suspiciously into the glass. Did this wine possess qualities I hadn't guessed at? 'Don't babble, Erskine-Brown.'

'"Nose," Rumpole! The bouquet. That's one of the expressions you have to learn to use about wine. Together with the length...'

'Length?' I looked down at the glass in my hand. The length seemed to be about one inch and shrinking rapidly.

'The length a great wine lingers in the mouth, Rumpole. Look, why don't you let me educate you? My friend Percy Prescott organizes tastings in the City. Terrifically good fun. You get to try about a dozen wines.'

'A dozen?' I was doubtful. 'An expensive business.'

'No, Rumpole. Free. Absolutely free. They are blind tastings.'

'You mean they make you blind drunk?' I couldn't resist asking. But the offer was not of the sort I felt able to refuse. 'Whoever this Prescott may be, Erskine-Brown,' I said, 'lead me to him.'

*   *   *   *

It was some time before Erskine-Brown made good his promise to improve my vinous education, but one lunchtime when neither of us had been able to pick up a customer in any sort of trouble with the law, my fellow barrister took me to the quiet premises of Prescott's Wine & Spirits Merchants in the City of London. After our credentials had been carefully checked we were shown into a small drinks party which had about it all the gaiety of an assembly of the bereaved when the corpse in question has left his entire fortune to the cats' home.

The meeting took place in a small, well-lit basement room. On a white, marble-topped table there were a number of bottles, all shrouded in brown paper bags taped up to their necks. Around the table the tasters twirled minute quantities of wine in their glasses, held them nervously up to the light, sniffed them with deep suspicion and finally allowed a small quantity to pass their lips.

They were surprisingly sober-looking characters in not surprisingly sober suits, one of which caught the eye. It was singularly well-cut and inside it was a tall, elegant creature with smooth fair hair, a haughtily aristocratic nose, and a single eyeglass, apparently held in place by surface tension, for it lacked both rim and cord. I recognized him, without benefit of my companion's whisper, from magazines in my dentist's waiting-room – Bertie Bellamy, the immensely rich taster and collector of fine wines. Only occasionally did a Texan tycoon, even richer, beat him at a Sotheby's wine auction to a pre-phylloxera first growth (whatever *that* may be: this arcane scrap of information *was* dredged from Erskine-Brown's aside.)

'What's the matter with you?' asked His Elegance. 'Can't you spit?'

I had just taken a swig of some smooth and velvety liquid that lingered in my mouth with a distant memory of wild strawberries (as Erskine-Brown might have said at one of his least tolerable moments). All I knew was that it was to Château Pommeroy what

59

a brief for Shell International in the House of Lords is to an indecent assault before the Uxbridge magistrates.

'Over there, in case you're looking for it. Expectoration corner!' Bertie waved me to a wooden wine-box, half-filled with sawdust, into which the gents in dark suitings were directing mouthfuls of purplish liquid. I moved away from him, reluctant to admit that such wine as I had been able to win had long since disappeared down the little red lane.

'Collie brought you, didn't he?' Prescott, the wine-merchant, caught me as I was about to swallow a second helping. He was a thin streak of a chap, in a dark suit and a stiff collar, whose faint smile, I thought, was thin-lipped and patronising.

'Collie?'

'Erskine-Brown. We called him Collie at school.'

'After the dog?' I saw my chambers companion insert the tip of his pale nose into the narrow top of his glass.

'No, after the Doctor – Collis-Browne. You know, Dr Collis Browne's Chlorodyne – good for schoolboy squitters. Not that that was the point, though Collie *was* a bit of a pill: it was double-barrelling a name like Brown! We used to kick him around at Winchester.'

Now I am far from saying that, in my long relationship with Claude Erskine-Brown, irritation has not sometimes got the better of me. But he is, after all, a long-time member of our chambers at Equity Court and as such has become as familiar and uncomfortable as the furniture. I resented the strictures of this public-school bully on my learned friend and was about to say so when the gloomy proceedings were interrupted by the arrival of an unlikely character wearing tartan trousers, rubber-soled canvas shoes of the type that I believe are generally known as 'trainers' and a zipped jacket that bore on its back the legend 'Monty Mantis Service Station. Luton. Beds'. Within it all was a squat, ginger-haired, youngish man who called out, 'Which way to the anti-freeze? At least we can get warmed up for the winter.' This was a clear reference to the recent scandal in the Austrian wine trade that was greeted, in the rarefied atmosphere of Prescott's tasting-room, with as much jollity as an advertisement for french letters would be in the Vatican.

'One of your customers?' I asked Prescott.

'One of my best,' he sighed. 'I imagine the profession of 'garagiste' in Luton must be extremely profitable. And he makes a point of coming to *all* our blind tastings.'

'Now I'm here,' Mr Mantis said, taking off his zipper jacket and displaying a yellow jumper ornamented with diamond lozenges, 'let battle commence.' He twirled and sniffed and took a mouthful from a tasting-glass, made a short but somehow revolting gargling sound and spat into the sawdust. 'A fairly unpretentious Côte-Rôtie,' he said as he did so. 'But on the whole 1975 was a disappointing year on the Rhône.'

The contest was run like a game of musical-chairs. They gave you a glass and if you guessed wrong, so to say, you were out and had to go and sit with the girls and have an ice-cream. At my first try I got that distant hint of wild strawberries again from a wine that was so far out of the usual run of my drinking that I became as tongue-tied as I would have done if I had been briefed in a highly lucrative claim for two and a half million on a bill of lading, and when asked to name the poison could only mutter, 'Damn good stuff,' and slink away from the field of battle. Erskine-Brown was knocked out in the second round, having confidently pronounced a Coonawarra to be Châteauneuf du Pape. 'Some bloody stuff from Wagga Wagga,' he grumbled – unreasonably, for on most occasions Claude was a staunch upholder of the Commonwealth. 'Shouldn't be allowed at a decent tasting!'

So we watched as, one by one, the contenders fell away. Prescott was in charge of the bottles and after the players had made their guesses he had finally to reveal the labels. From time to time, in the manner of donnish quiz-masters on up-market wireless guessing games, he would give little hints, particularly if he liked the contender. 'A churchyard number' might indicate a Graves, or a 'macabre little item, somewhat skeletal' was Beaune, he would explain to the politely smiling assembly. He never, I noticed, gave much assistance to the garagiste from Luton, nor did he need to, because the ebullient Mr Monty Mantis had no difficulty in identifying his wines and could even make a decent stab at the vintage, although perfect accuracy in that respect wasn't required in the game.

Finally the challengers were reduced to two, Monty Mantis, and the haughty creature with the eyeglass – Bertie, as he was known to all the pin-striped expectorating undertakers around him. It was their bottoms that hovered, figuratively speaking, over the final chair, the last parcelled bottle. Prescott was holding this with particular reverence as he poured a taster into two glasses. Monty

Mantis regarded the colour, lowered his nose to the level of the tide, took a mouthful and spat rapidly.

'Gordon Bennet!' He seemed to be somewhat amazed. 'Don't want to risk swallowing that. It might ruin me carburettor!'

Prescott looked pale and extremely angry. He turned to the other contestant, who was swilling the stuff around his dentures in a far more impressive way. 'Well, Bertie,' he said as he spat neatly, 'let me give you a clue. It's not whisky.'

'I think I could tell that.' He looked impassive. 'Not whisky.'

'But think...Just think...' Prescott seemed anxious to bring the contest to a rapid end by helping him. 'Think of a whisky translated.'

'Le quatre-star Esso?' said the garagiste, but Prescott was unamused.

'White Horse?' Bertie frowned.

'Very good. Something conservative, of course. And keep to the right!'

'The right bank of the river? St. Emilion...White Horse? Cheval Blanc...' Bertie arrived at his destination with a certain amount of doubt.

'Nineteen-seventy one, I'm afraid, nothing earlier.' Prescott was pulling away the brown paper to reveal a label on which the words 'Cheval Blanc' and 'Appellation St. Emilion Controlée' were to be clearly read. There was a smatter of applause. 'Dear old Bertie! Still an unbeatable palate.' It was applause in which the Luton garagiste didn't join, but he was laughing as Prescott turned to him and said, icily polite, 'I'm sorry you were pipped at the post, Mr Mantis. You did jolly well. Now, Bertie, if you'll once again accept the certificate of Les Grands Contestants du Vin and the complimentary bottle which this time is a magnum of Gevrey Chambertin Clair-Paü 1970 – a somewhat underrated vintage. Can you not stay with us, Mr Mantis?'

But Monty Mantis was on his way to the door, muttering something about getting himself decarbonized. Nobody laughed, and no one seemed particularly sorry to see him go.

*   *   *   *

Nothing changes in this life, and many months later I was back in my usual embarrassing position before His Honour Judge Roger

Bullingham defending a certain Freddy 'Fingers' O'Keefe on a charge of receiving stolen property. I mention this in connection with my visit to the wine-tasting only because the property concerned this time in Freddy's difficulties was a collection of fine wines, locked up as exhibits in the police room at the side of the court. And the loser, the innocent victim of the crime on this particular occasion, was Mr Percy Prescott who had given poor old Claude Erskine-Brown such a terrible time at Winchester.

The old Wykehamist bully and I bandied words in a general way for a while and I discovered him to be an intelligent witness, rather over-anxious to defend himself against any imagined attack. When I had lulled him into a false sense of security with a string of harmless questions I came to the heart of the matter.

'Mr Prescott. How long have you been in the wine business?'

'I opened my present shop just three years ago.'

'And before that?'

'Before that I was selling pictures. I had a shop in Chelsea. We specialised in nineteenth-century water-colours, my Lord.'

'Did you ever have occasion to make an insurance claim in connection with that business?' I carefully sought for and found a sheet of paper which I hoped the witness might think contained details of his past; in fact it was a brutally phrased reminder that my subscription to Her Majesty's Government's funds was now overdue. The old trick worked and Mr Percy Prescott was persuaded to tell the truth.

'We had a serious break-in and most of our stock was taken. Of course I had to make a claim.'

'You seem to be somewhat prone to serious break-ins, Mr Prescott?'

'It's the rising tide of lawlessness.' There came a menacing rumble from the learned judge. 'Which is threatening to engulf us all! You should know that better than anyone, Mister Rumpole.' The Mad Bull was staring at me as though I were personally responsible for all the break-ins the unfortunate Prescott had ever suffered. To avoid his somewhat bloodshot and accusing eye I asked the Usher to arrange for one of the exhibits, to wit a bottle of the Cheval Blanc, to be brought into court.

'Mr Prescott, you say this bottle contains vintage claret of a high quality?'

'Yes.'

'Retailing at what price?'

'I think, around fifty pounds a bottle.'

'And insured for...?'

'I believe we insured it for the retail price. Such a wine would be very hard to replace.'

'Of course it would, Mr Rumpole!' The old expert on the bench was rebuking me as usual. 'It's a particularly fine vintage of the...what did you say it was?'

'Cheval Blanc, my Lord.'

'And we all know what you have to pay for good burgundy nowadays.' His Honour Judge Bullingham looked to the jury for support, but as most of them were black and unemployed and came from Tower Hamlets they looked back at him somewhat blankly.

'It's a claret, my Lord. Not a burgundy,' the witness was foolish enough to remind him.

'A claret? Yes, of course. Didn't I say that?' The Bull was not pleased. 'Carry on, Mr Rumpole.'

'My Lord. I have an application to make in respect of this exhibit.'

'Very well.' The Bull sighed heavily and closed his eyes, but I kept my application short. 'I wish,' I said, 'to open this alleged bottle of Château Cheval Blanc.'

'For what purpose, Mr Rumpole?'

'For the purpose of tasting it, my Lord.'

Slowly, from the cutting edge of his stiff white collar to the lower fringes of his dirty white wig the Bull changed colour and his face became a deeper shade of purple. 'This is a court of law, Mr Rumpole,' he reminded me somewhat unnecessarily. 'This is not a bar! I have sat here for a long time, for far too long in my opinion, listening to your cross-examination of this unfortunate gentleman who has, as the jury may well find, suffered at the hands of your client, but I do not intend to sit here, Mr Rumpole, while you drink the exhibits.'

'Not drink. "Taste", my Lord. I fully intend to spit it out. And may I say this. If the defence is to be denied the opportunity of inspecting a vital exhibit, *that* would be a breach of our fundamental liberties, the principles we have fought for since the days of Magna Carta! And I should have to make an immediate application to the Court of Appeal.'

The Bull paled a little beneath his purple flush. If there's one thing that frightens Judge Bullingham it's the Court of Appeal which, given half a chance, is apt to pour a good deal of quiet scorn on some of his more hasty decisions. In the end the usher was sent up to the judges' dining-room and returned with a corkscrew and glasses for both counsel and the judge. When I lifted the alleged Cheval Blanc '71 to my lips I was not altogether unprepared. I had, in the days before the trial, taken the precaution of visiting Luton and having a long chat with the garagiste. It seems that Monty Mantis had been taken on a school trip to Dieppe at the age of twelve, and the bottle of wine he had secretly bought with his pocket money had given him a private passion that took the place of other lads' interest in football, film stars or homing pigeons. Since that first, unforgettable glass he had spent much time and money on turning himself into a genuine and undeniable expert. I trusted the judgement of Monty Mantis, and yet, all the same, it came as a considerable relief, as I sipped Exhibit P.1. in court, to encounter the rough, rasping, familiar, not to say over-familiar, taste of the usual plonk of a penurious Old Bailey hack, something closely akin to Château Thames Embankment. Even the Bull got the point.

'Are you saying, Mr Rumpole, that this claret is not what it pretends to be?'

'Exactly, my Lord. I shall be calling expert evidence. Mr Bellamy, whom you will know as probably our greatest connoisseur of clarets...'

'But what exactly are you suggesting? If Mr Prescott were to sell this as highly expensive, vintage claret the deceit would be obvious to anyone drinking...'

'I am not suggesting that this wine was in Mr Prescott's possession for drinking, my Lord.'

'Then what was it in his possession for?'

I turned to look at the collapsed figure in the witness box. Percy Prescott had paled and his forehead looked damp, his collar also seemed several sizes too small for him. I would have felt sorrier for him if he hadn't kicked poor old Erskine-Brown at school.

'He had it for stealing, my Lord.'

* * * *

'Of course, Prescott fixed the burglary at his wine shop as he had fixed the stealing of his alleged Victorian water-colours. There was a considerable profit margin on the cost of filling those bottles with plonk and the value he put on the insurance claim. I imagine he had some real Cheval Blanc on the premises and the bottles put out for the "blind" tasting got confused.' I was giving an account of my triumph in R v O'Keefe to Erskine-Brown as we sat in our favourite watering-hole. 'He must have been in a terrible sweat when he realised he'd given Monty Mantis a mouthful of the rough stuff to taste.'

'You mean Prescott *organized* the burglary?'

'Of course. He'd had a bit of practice when he sold Victorian water-colours. He paid whoever it was to dispose of the stuff on some rubbish tip where the bottles could be broken up and hidden. Instead it got sold round the pubs and Freddy took an investment.'

'But isn't that receiving stolen property?' Claude Erskine-Brown is chronically prosecution-minded.

'It was never stolen property. It was removed with the owner's consent. I know the law, old darling.'

'Do you, Rumpole? I never thought you did. Only one thing I can't understand...'

'What?'

'Why on earth did your expert, Bertie Bellamy, not recognize the stuff at the blind tasting. He was quite clear about it in court.'

'I think he did, or he had serious doubts. But Prescott had given him what he thought was the answer he needed to win. One other thing – he just couldn't accept the fact that Monty Mantis knew as much as he did about wine. He wore that terrible anorak, you see. And he kept a garage in Luton. I tell you what, Claude, people pay far too much attention to the label on the bottle. Well, here's to crime.'

I raised my glass and filled my mouth with Pommeroy's Very Ordinary. It would be a long time, I knew, before I got another distant hint of the flavour of wild strawberries.

Sherry: a Story

Peter Fleming

I T won't do,' said Freddie Korn moodily. His cigarette, half-smoked, dropped into the cuspidor beside him with a disgruntled hiss.

'Pity,' said Mr. Lather. They were silent for a moment.

Then 'Run through that last coupla hundred feet again,' Korn barked over his shoulder. As the lights in the projection-room went down he lit another cigarette.

The darkness began to whirr. Flick! On the screen before them was an apartment, rich, discreet, faintly Cubist. Through the window, the roof-tops of New York at night, tapering honeycombs of light, effectively haphazard. ('Fake?' queried Mr. Lather. 'No. Stuff I didn't use in *Fallen*,' Korn grunted.) In the apartment a man in evening dress shakes a cocktail, smiling, while a gramophone is delivered of a waltz. The telephone rings. He stops the gramophone, moves to answer it. 'Ask her to come right up.'...A knock. He opens the door. A girl frames herself in it – blonde, lovely, terrific in a hundredweight of furs. They shake hands....

Dialogue: slick, insistent, economically outlining a situation. She questions. He evades: lies clumsily: is cornered: confesses. Her face, huge, incredulous, outraged. 'With *Sylvia*! My God! You took my kid sister to a joint like that!...' One hand, in the approved style, is at her throat. With the other, swiftly drawn back, she flings the contents of her cocktail-glass in his face. Dazed, hurt, wronged, his dripping features monopolize the screen, angling for sympathy; the audience must understand that this man is Not All Bad. His white tie droops, disproportionately bedraggled....

'O.K. That's all I want.' Freddie Korn's petulant incisive voice sounded oddly after the disembodied mouthings of the talkie. The whirring stopped. The lights went up.

'I think I get what you mean,' said Mr. Lather diffidently. He respected Freddie, and knew his value as a director to Stupor Mundi (Inc.). 'You want something more pictorially effective than the dope in that cocktail. It lets the climax down. He gets a good wetting, but he ought to be in more of a mess.'

'The custard-pie touch,' said Korn drily. 'But you're right, Mr. Lather. I guess we'll shoot that sequence over again first thing tomorrow; and we'll use sherry instead of the cocktail. Dark sherry.'

'But would smart guys like that be drinking sherry?'

'In New York? Hell, it's *dernier cri*. Old English custom, and all that. By the time this picture's released the great American public will just about have gotten to hear of it. Like the backgammon craze, you know.'

'Oh,' said Mr. Lather. Freddie moved in social circles beyond his ken. Mrs. Lather would be interested to hear that sherry was going to be fashionable.

*   *   *

Crogan had worked in the Stupor Mundi Studios for nearly a year now. His friends told him that he was lucky to get the job; they did not expect him to keep it. Crogan drank. He was a queer fellow, an Irishman, with a chalky-white face and stiff black hair which stood up on his forehead *en brosse* and looked as if it never grew. It was a square, jutting little face like a dog's. Pale blue eyes, small and hostile, met you when you glanced at it, warning you off, so that the most casual glance stood convicted as a stare. People, as a matter of fact, were apt to stare at Crogan. There was an unnatural intensity about his pallor under the cap of fierce black hair. It was so complete, so unrelieved. Instinctively, but in vain, you looked for a touch of blue about the jowls, a shadow on the upper lip. That tight, smooth skin suggested at once a clown and a corpse.

He was not, and did not deserve to be, popular. He was a secret man, inscrutable and ulterior as a cat; not just aloof, keeping his distance firmly, definably; but always edging away, furtive, ungracious; avoiding, not rejecting, the world around him.

There had been a time when he was certain of employment for three or four months in the year. There was a theatre in New York where they used to put on a repertory of plays for children in the winter – pantomimes of a sort, with fairies on wires and transformation scenes. Crogan used to play the animal parts – the hero's cat, or the King Wolf, or a friendly bear. He was uncannily good at them, achieving and sustaining a suggestion of realism which the children (who are never satisfied with the usual perfunctory, shambling stage fauna) adored and remembered. It was Crogan's one accomplishment, and he enjoyed doing it. Doubled up, sweating, raking his throat with uncouth noises, he heard the children's laughter, saw, through the gauze-covered eye-holes in his stifling mask, the flicker of small applauding hands beyond the footlights, and was content. It was a queer recipe for happiness, but Crogan never came near finding another. Perhaps that was why he retained, even after he drank himself out of that job, some hint of the loved mimicry in his bearing. Was it in his gait, or in his figure, or rooted deeper in the man himself? You could not, when you came to think of it, be sure. But somehow, when you heard that Crogan had once played animal parts superlatively well, you were not surprised; it was as if you had been given a clue to something baffling and arresting in your impression of the man.

Crogan was attached to the Property Room in the Stupor Mundi Studios, the least of many assistants. It was not a good job. Work on the production of a film is an affair of sickening redundancy. Scenes are taken and retaken till the substance of them acquires the ludicrous, exasperating improbability of a word written over and over again on a blank sheet of paper. It was Crogan's business to see that all the minor, perishable properties – cigarettes, food, seals on letters, folded newspapers, blank cartridges – which were consumed, destroyed, or disarranged in the shooting of a scene were replaced immediately, ready for a retake. It was work which called for a wearisome attention to detail, but Crogan did not mind that. What he resented, and at last came to dread, was the element of repetition it grafted on to his life. He was there to put the finishing touches, yet the nature of his work mocked at finality. It entailed long loitering, with no predictable end; irksome because it was vaguely purposeful. Day after day, hour after hour, Crogan would be standing in the silent group of men round the cameras while in the brightly-lit angle of two roofless walls men and women with yellow faces and green eye-lids repeated words and recaptured grimaces till both had lost their slender relevance in repetition. They would break off for no apparent reason. An electric bell would shrill through the studios, releasing them from the petrifying domination of the microphone. Speech and movement would be resumed, and Crogan would go wearily forward to empty an ashtray, retard the hands of a clock, and restore ravished cushions to respectability.

It was an unnatural life. Sun and moon were in the control of the electrician, and the hours travelled incalculably through all this redundancy, like an army through a forest. In Crogan's dark, unsteady mind it bred confusion, and a blurred anger. Sometimes he mistook his lunch-interval for the end of the day's work; it shook him to find the sun high over the city instead of twilight with its welcome implications. With his sense of time he began to lose his grip on his own personality. Queer, wild thoughts came crowding into his head as he watched the stale and meaningless bustle on the sets. In a kind of waking dream he encountered a new Crogan – a man of power, an avenger, capable of giving worthy expression to the sullen, objectless hatred which he had come to recognize as dominating his soul.

One day his hatred found an object, his life an ambition. He was working for Freddie Korn on a picture which he vaguely knew was called *The Taunt*; it seemed to be concerned with fast life in New York. Gerald Flattery was starred, with Virginia Raikes. The first big scene to be shot was the cocktail-throwing scene.

Gerald Flattery was in a vile temper that morning. He had been on a party the night before. The scriptgirls, cheated of his mechanical largesse of smiles, commented acidly on his notoriously weak head. Freddie Korn looked dubious. A hangover made Gerald slack and intractable.

'We'll just run through the business and dialogue again before we start shooting,' he announced.

Crogan looked at his plot of the set. Gramophone wound up; cocktail-shaker full; two glasses; cigarettes – all O.K. He sighed and withdrew to his dreams, ignoring the rattle of dialogue.

Presently it stopped unexpectedly. There was an interruption.

'Hey!' Gerald Flattery was protesting; 'you don't need to chuck that stuff over me, Virginia. It's only a run-through. She needn't, need she, Freddie?'

'But I want to check up on the business, Mr. Korn. We never did it last night. It's not so darned easy to shoot a thimble-full of liquor across the set as if I meant it.' Virginia and Gerald got on badly together.

'Aw, hell! I'm not going to ruin my make-up at rehearsal.'

'Well, I don't care what happens, so long as I have a target.'

Freddie Korn made a tired gesture.

'One of you boys go out on the set and stand over where Mr. Flattery stands.'

There was no scramble for the distinction of being publicly soused, even by radiance in a hundredweight of furs. The group of men round the cameras stood frozen in deprecating, faintly competitive reluctance.

'Here, you!' Gerald strode over to where Crogan's face stood out, white and luminous, in the reflected glare of innumerable watts. 'You'll do. If that's not a target on the front of your skull I don't know what it is. He slapped Crogan on the back. 'See where I was standing?'

'Yes,' said Crogan.

'Well, go and stand there. Open your mouth and shut your eyes and Miss Raikes'll give you a hell of a surprise.'

Crogan went. He had four consecutive glasses of ginger ale thrown in his face before Virginia and Freddie were satisfied with the venom in her gesture. He was dimly aware that everyone was laughing at him: that they laughed rather more every time it was done. The only face he saw was Gerald Flattery's, consciously patronizing the common mockery. The only laugh he heard was high-pitched, trailing disdain without amusement....

In Crogan's heart a new purpose came into existence. His hatred welcomed the image of Gerald Flattery as embers welcome a fresh log, licking it hungrily, searing it. The others saw only a man who spluttered ludicrously, and wiped his face with the back of his sleeve in a careful, feline gesture. It made it all the funnier, that he was so obviously angry. They roared with laughter. They could not see that he was half mad with rage.

Two days later Crogan saw, and grasped, a devious fragile strand of opportunity.

Kaplan, a Jew, was in charge of the Property room. Crogan, alone of the men there, got no share of his studied and bounteous geniality. He could not play down to Crogan. He was frightened of him.

It was late. Most people had gone, and the studios, ill-lit, wore for once the air of spacious dinginess which was truly theirs. They could no longer borrow a bright, vicarious intimacy from new sets enfiladed with light. Odd bits of rope hung wistfully from the gaunt, ribbed roof. Underground, in the carpenter's shop, beat the forlorn pulse of a belated hammer. A ribald laugh filtered faintly down from the dressing-rooms. Kaplan was leaning against a pillar near the main door.

Crogan, summoned, came to him from behind, walking very quietly in the rubber-soled shoes he always wore.

'Thinks I don't hear him,' Kaplan told himself irritably. Crogan always made him unreasonable. 'Listen, Crogan,' he said roughly (not turning his head, so that Crogan should know how perfectly audible his approach had been.) 'There's a retake scheduled for 9.30 to-morrow morning on No. 6 set. It's that scene they shot a coupla days ago – dame throwing liquor in a guy's face. Remember?'

'Sure,' said Crogan quietly.

Kaplan guffawed. 'I'll say you remember. Well, they've just run it through in the projection-room, and Freddie Korn's not happy about the dope we used in that cocktail. Doesn't photograph well: not enough mess. He wants us to fake up something to look like sherry.'

'Sherry?'

'Yeah. Dark, sticky sort of a wine. You'd better get some milk and put that colouring stuff in it; that'll show up all right. And ask Matt for one of those decanters they were using on No. 4 last week.'

'You won't be here, Mr. Kaplan?'

'No. Baumer's got me working on that comic upstairs. This is your job, Crogan. And if you go and mess it up they'll come down on me. So be around here good and early, and don't get sozzled to-night. See!'

'O.K., Mr. Kaplan.'

Crogan padded away in the shadows. Kaplan, watching him go,

thought he noticed something springy, a hint of elation, in his quick furtive steps. 'That guy's stepping out as if I'd given him a rise,' thought the Jew, with regret for harshnesses withheld.

Coming out next morning, Crogan kept himself more than ever aloof from his fellow-passengers. He had need to. His right hand, thrust deep in his overcoat pocket, clutched a small dark blue bottle containing vitriol. There was a queer, stiff little grin on his face. His pale eyes flickered mischievously. Their comprehensive hostility had left them.

He bought some milk at a drug-store on his way from the station, darting contemptuous, triumphant glances at the commuters who wolfed hurried breakfasts at the counter. Poor, ignoble stuff, mankind seemed to him to-day. He could afford to spurn, not shun it. The stiff little grin still framed his mouth when he reached the studios.

Matt, the Swede, and another man were down in the Property Room, smoking and laughing and feeding pea-nuts to some rabbits which were being used in the comic upstairs. Crogan nodded to them and went to a sink at the far end. He found the decanter and mixed milk, water, and colouring fluid till he had a basin full of rich, chocolate-coloured liquid. From it he half-filled the decanter. Then he looked over his shoulder. The rabbits, fastidious, disorientated, were still amusing Matt and the other man. Their backs were turned. Their laughter loitered down the room. Crogan sighed happily and drew the dark blue bottle from his pocket. Then he poured the vitriol into the decanter.

The fears of ignorance went unrealized. There was no steam, no bubbles, no hissing froth to crack the foundations of his plan. The heavy, opaque liquid still glumly counterfeited sherry. Crogan gave a grunt of satisfaction, put the decanter on a tray, and padded upstairs.

Freddie Korn was on the set already.

'This what you want, Mr. Korn?' Crogan asked him, conscious for the first time of a suffocating anxiety.

The decanter was inspected thoughtfully.

'O.K.,' said Freddie Korn, 'that's the goods. How d'you make it?'

Crogan told him three of the ingredients and put the tray lovingly on its appointed table. Then he looked to his other properties and withdrew.

Gerald Flattery was punctual. Crogan, following his casual grace across the set with greedy, excited eyes, saw that he was in a good temper.

'Gosh!' he said, when he saw the decanter, 'Stupor Mundi's going to have a hell of a bill for boiled shirts from me.'

The script-girls tittered sycophantically. ('That's right. Laugh at him,' thought Crogan. He felt full of gaiety himself. There was, now, something extraordinarily funny about that smooth, dark man accepting homage for his face.)

Virginia Raikes was late. She usually was, and Crogan knew it. He suffered, nevertheless, five minutes' acute despondency. His exultation left him, and drained off some of his sustaining hatred. Unused to endeavour, he was startled and appalled to find how bitter was the thought of failure. But at last she arrived, and tripped off, in apologetic but becoming haste, to her dressing-room. Crogan wanted to shout his relief.

Five more minutes and everything was ready. Freddie Korn, hunched on his camp-stool in a characteristic compromise between tension and indolence, gave his last orders.

'You won't forget to say "a glass of sherry" and not "a cocktail"?'

'Not on your life,' said Gerald Flattery, with one of his facile, devastating smiles.

'O.K. Let's go,' grunted Korn, and pressed a button at his side.

The warning bell dinned through the studios, a quivering blade of sound, shearing through speech and action like a knife. Movements were suspended or postponed, cautiously and at once. All over the floor men put things down and stood still, staring patiently at nothing. As the admonitory echoes died, silence closed down on them like a lid. The two microphones on Set No. 6 dangled inertly – unobtrusive tyrants. The three sound-proof boxes enclosing cameras began to whir.

Crogan watched the set as he had never watched a set before. Flayed by the arc-lights, it stood empty for a moment. Then the door opened and Gerald Flattery came in, whistling. From then on Crogan saw his face and nothing else. The sound of the gramophone, the telephone, Virginia Raikes's flamboyant entrance – these things did not touch his consciousness. For him the world held nothing but a poised profile, specious eyes, a smugly handsome mouth: that face and the march of the minutes....The dialogue rattle on unheeded, like rain on the window beside a man asleep. Crogan's grin widened, showing his white and pointed teeth.

'A glass of sherry.' The words numbed and concentrated his mind as the bell had numbed and concentrated the studio. Only a few seconds now....Crogan's triumph welled within him, as palpable as physical nausea. He had tasted no moment like this before. Savage amusement flared in his pale-blue eyes. His lips were drawn back. He was grinning like a man in agony. He was beside himself....

'With *Sylvia*! My God! You took my kid sister to –'

Crogan lost control. A screech of laughter, like a thrown spear, cleft the attentive silence; then another, and another, and another. Wild, slashing yells of mirth, far divorced from human laughter, volleyed in men's ears. Action stopped on the set. Freddie Korn pressed the button at his side and the bell, sardonically official, released the studio from a spell already broken.

Everyone stared at Crogan: everyone except Freddie Korn. He was looking at the table on which Virginia had replaced, unsteadily, the glass of faked sherry. Some had been spilt. Where the drops had fallen little malignant beads of froth were active on the painted wood.

'Lock that man up in my room,' he said; and they took Crogan away.

A Story to Tell, 1942

The Three Low Masses:
a Christmas Story

Alphonse Daudet

I

'TWO truffled turkeys, Garrigou?'

'Yes, your Reverence, two magnificent turkeys stuffed with truffles. I know, because I helped stuff them. The skin had been stretched so tightly you would have thought it was going to burst as it was roasting...'

'Jesus-Maria! How I do love truffles! Give me my surplice. Quickly, Garrigou...And what else did you see in the kitchen, besides the turkeys?...'

'Oh, all sorts of good things ... Since midday they've done nothing but pluck pheasants, larks, pullets, grouse. Feathers flying everywhere ... Then they brought eels, carp, trout from the pond and...

'How big – the trout, Garrigou?'

'As big as that, your Reverence...Enormous!'

'Merciful heavens! You make me see them ... Have you put the wine in the altar-cruets?'

'Yes, your Reverence, I've put the wine in the altar-cruets ... But you wait and see! It doesn't compare with what you'll be drinking soon, after Midnight Mass. You should see inside the dining-room at the château: decanters blazing bright with wines of all colours ... And the silver dishes, the carved dining-table, the flowers, the candelabra! ... Never will there be a Christmas midnight supper like it. Monsieur le Marquis has invited all the nobility of the neighbourhood. You will be at least forty at table, not counting the bailiff and the scrivener. Ah, you are indeed fortunate to be among them, your Reverence! Just from having sniffed those beautiful turkeys, the smell of the truffles is following me everywhere...Myum!...'

'Come now, my son. Let us guard ourselves against the sin of gluttony, especially on the eve of the Nativity...Off with you, quickly. Light the candles and ring the bell for the first Mass; it is nearly midnight already, and we mustn't be late...'

This conversation took place one Christmas Eve in the year of grace sixteen hundred and something, between the Reverend Father Balaguère, formerly Prior of the Barnabites, at present Chaplain to the Lords of Trinquelage, and his little clerk Garrigou, for you must know that the devil, on that very evening, had assumed the round face and nondescript features of the young sacristan, the better to lead the reverend father into temptation and make him commit the terrible sin of gluttony. So, whilst the supposed Garrigou (Hem! hm!) was vigorously jingling the bells of the baronial chapel, the reverend father was hastening to clothe himself in his chasuble in the little sacristy of the château and, already troubled in spirit by all these gastronomic descriptions, he was repeating to himself as he dressed,

'Roast turkeys...golden carp...trout as big as that!...'

Outside, the night wind was blowing, spreading the music of the bells, and gradually lights were appearing in the darkness along the slopes of Mont Ventoux, on the top of which rose the age-old towers of Trinquelage. The families of the tenant-farmers were coming to hear Midnight Mass at the château. They sang as they climbed the incline in groups of five or six, the father in front, lantern in hand, the women swathed in their long, brown cloaks under which the children huddled for shelter. In spite of the hour and the cold, all these good folk walked cheerfully, sustained by the thought that when they came out from Mass there would be tables laid for them down in the kitchens, as there were every year. Now and then, on the steep slope, a nobleman's carriage preceded by torch bearers would twinkle its windows in the moonlight, or a mule would trot along tinkling its bells, and by the light of the mist-enveloped lanterns, the tenants would recognize their bailiff and salute him as he passed.

'Good evening, good evening, Master Arnoton!'

'Good evening, good evening, friends!'

The night was clear, the stars gleamed bright in the cold air; the north wind and a fine frozen snow, glancing off the clothes without wetting them, faithfully maintained the tradition of a white Christmas. At the very summit of the slope rose their destination, the château, with its enormous mass of towers and gables, its chapel spire rising into the bluish-black sky, and, at all its windows, little lights that twinkled, bobbing back and forth, and looking, against the dark background of the building, like sparks flashing in the ashes of burnt paper...Once one was beyond the drawbridge and the postern-gate, to reach the chapel it was necessary to cross the outer courtyard, full of carriages, valets and sedan chairs, all brightly lit by the flames of torches and by the blazing kitchen fires. All around could be heard the chinking click of the turnspits, the clatter of pans, the clink of crystal and silver being set out in preparation for a feast; from up above, a warm vapour which smelt of roast meat and potent herbs used for complicated sauces made not only the tenants, but the chaplain, the bailiff, everybody, say:

'What a fine Christmas supper we are going to have after Mass!'

II

Dingdong-dong!...Dingdong-dong!...

So the Midnight Mass begins. In the chapel of the château, a cathedral in miniature, with interlaced arches and oak wainscoting high up the walls, tapestries have been hung, all the candles lit. And the people! The costumes! See first, seated in the carved stalls surrounding the chancel, the Lord of Trinquelage, in salmon-coloured taffeta, and near him all the invited nobility. Opposite, kneeling on prie-Dieus hung with velvet, are the old Dowager Marchioness in her gown of flame-coloured brocade and the young Lady of Trinquelage, wearing on her head the latest fashion of the Court of France: a high tower of fluted lace. Further back, their faces shaved, and wearing black with vast pointed wigs, can be seen the bailiff Thomas Arnoton and the scrivener Master Ambroy, striking two solemn notes among the gaudy silks and brocaded damasks. Then come the fat major domos, the pages, the grooms, the stewards, the housekeeper with all her keys hung at her side on a fine silver chain. Further back, on benches, are the servants, the maids, and the tenants with their families. And last of all, at the very back, right against the door which they open and shut discreetly, are the scullions who slip in, between sauces, to snatch a little of the atmosphere of the Mass and to bring the smell of the supper into the church, festive and warm with all its lighted candles.

Is it the sight of the scullions' little white caps which distracts the officiating priest? Might it not rather be Garrigou's little bell, that mocking little bell which shakes at the foot of the altar with such infernal haste and seems to keep saying:

'Let's hurry! Let's hurry! The sooner we're finished, the sooner we'll be at supper.'

The fact is that each time this devilish little bell rings, the chaplain forgets his Mass and thinks only of the midnight supper. He imagines the scurrying cooks, the kitchen stoves blazing like blacksmiths' forges, the steam escaping from half-open lids, and, beneath that steam, two magnificent turkeys, stuffed, taut, bursting with truffles...

Or still more, he sees pages passing in files carrying dishes surrounded with tempting odours, and he goes with them into the great hall already prepared for the feast. Oh, paradise! He sees the immense table blazing with lights and laden from end to end with peacocks dressed in their feathers, pheasants spreading their wings, flagons the colour of rubies, fruit dazzling bright among green branches, and all the marvellous fish Garrigou was talking about (yes! – Garrigou, of course) displayed on a bed of fennel, their scales pearly as if just from the sea, with bunches of sweet-smelling herbs in their huge nostrils. So real is the vision of these marvels that it seems to Father Balaguère that all these wonderful dishes are served before him on the embroidered altar-cloth, and once – or twice, instead of 'Dominus vobiscum!' he catches himself saying 'Benedicite'. Apart from these slight mistakes, the worthy man recites his office most conscientiously, without missing a line, without omitting one genuflection, and all goes very well until the end of the first Mass; for, as you know, the same priests must celebrate three consecutive Masses on Christmas Day.

'One over!' says the chaplain to himself with a sigh of relief; then, without wasting a moment, he signs to his clerk, or him whom he thinks is his clerk, and—

Dingdong-dong!...Dingdong-dong!...

So the second Mass begins, and with it begins also the sin of Father Balaguère.

'Quick, quick, let's hurry!' Garrigou's little bell cries to him in its shrill little voice, and this time the unfortunate priest abandons himself completely to the demon of gluttony, hurls himself on the missal and devours the pages with the avidity of his over-stimulated appetite. Frantically he kneels, rises, makes vague signs of the cross, half-genuflects, cuts short all his gestures in order to finish the sooner. He scarcely extends his arms at the Gospel, or beats his breast at the *Confiteor*. It is between the clerk and himself who will jabber the quicker. Verses and responses patter pell-mell, buffeting each other. Words half-pronounced without opening the mouth, which would take too much time, die away in a baffling hum.

'*Oremus ps...ps...ps...*'

'*Mea culpa...pa...pa...*'

Like hurrying wine-harvesters treading the grapes, both splatter about in the latin of the Mass, sending splashes in all directions.

'*Dom...scum!...,*' says Balaguère.

'*...Stutuo...,*' replies Garrigou; and all the time that damned little bell is ringing in their ears, like those bells they put on post-horses to make them gallop quicker. Obviously at this pace a Low Mass is quickly got out of the way.

'Two over!' says the chaplain quite out of breath; then, red and sweating, without pausing to recover, he rushes down the altar steps and...

Ding-dong!...Dingdong-dong!...

So the third Mass begins. It is not far now to the dining hall; but, alas, the nearer the midnight supper approaches, the more the unfortunate Balaguère feels himself seized by a gluttonous mad-ness of impatience. He even sees more distinctly the golden carp, the roast turkeys...There!... Yes, and there!...He touches them... he...Oh, merciful heavens!... the dishes are steaming, the wines are ambrosial, and, shaking itself madly, the little bell is shrieking at him:

'Quick, quick! Be more quick!'

But how could he go more quickly? His lips are scarcely moving. He is no longer pronouncing the words...Unless he cheats the good God completely and omits part of the Mass...And that is exactly what the wretched man does! Falling deeper into temptation, he begins by skipping one verse, then two. Then the Epistle is too long so he doesn't finish it; he skims through the Gospel, passes over the Creed, jumps the Pater, bows distantly to the Preface, and thus by leaps and bounds hurls himself into eternal damnation, closely fol-lowed by the infamous Garrigou (*vade, retro, Satanus!*) who co-operates splendidly, holding up his chasuble, turning the pages two at a time, knocking over the desks, upsetting the altar-cruets, and ceaselessly shaking that tiny little bell, louder and louder, quicker and quicker.

The startled faces of the congregation are a sight to behold! Obliged to join in a Mass conducted in dumb-show by a priest whose words they can't hear, some stand up as others are kneeling, or sit when others are rising. And every succeeding part of this extraordinary service results in a confused variety of postures on all the benches. The Star of the Nativity, journeying up there across the sky towards the little stable, paled with apprehension at the sight of such disorder.

'The priest is going too quickly ... you can't keep up with him,' the old Dowager grumbles, shaking her coif angrily.

Master Arnoton, his large steel spectacles on his nose, searches in his prayer-book, wondering where the deuce they are up to. But, on the whole, all these worthy folk are themselves also thinking of the supper, and are not sorry the Mass is going at top speed. And when

Father Balaguère, his face shining radiantly, turns towards the congregation and shouts at the top of his voice: '*Ite, missa est,*' the whole chapel replies, as one voice, with a '*Deo Gratias*' so merry and so lively you would have thought they were already at table responding to the first toast.

III

Five minutes later, all the nobles were taking their seats in the great hall, the chaplain in the midst of them. The château, bright with lights in every room, was reverberating with songs, shouts, laughter, uproar everywhere; and the venerable Father Balaguère was plunging his fork into the wing of the grouse, drowning remorse for his sin under floods of wine and rich meat gravy. The unfortunate holy man drank so much and ate so much, he died of a stroke that night without even having time to repent. In the morning, he arrived in heaven still all in a stupor after the night's feasting and I leave you to ponder over the reception he was given.

'Get out of My sight, you wicked Christian!' the Sovereign Judge, Master of us all, said to him, 'Your lapse from virtue is so great it outweighs all the goodness of your life. You stole from Me a Midnight Mass. Well, you will pay it back three-hundred-fold. You will not enter Paradise until you have celebrated three hundred Christmas Masses in your own chapel and in the presence of all those who sinned with you and by your fault.'

...Such, in truth, is the legend of Father Balaguère, as you will hear it told in the land of olives. Today the Château de Trinquelage no longer exists, but the chapel still stands on the summit of Mont Ventoux, in a clump of holly oaks. Its disjointed door bangs in the wind, its threshold is overgrown with weeds; there are nests in the corners of the altar and in the recesses of the huge casement windows from which the coloured glass has long since disappeared. Yet it is said that at Christmas every year a supernatural light hovers among these ruins, and that peasants, going to Mass and the midnight supper in the church since built below, see this ghost of a chapel lit with invisible candles which burn in the open air even in wind and snow. You may laugh if you will, but a local vine-grower named Garrigue, a descendant no doubt of Garrigou, has assured me that one Christmas Eve, being slightly drunk, he had lost his way on the mountain near Trinquelage; and this is what he saw ... Until eleven o'clock, nothing. Suddenly, towards midnight, a peal of bells sounded high in the steeple, an old peal not heard for many many years and seeming to come from many leagues away. Soon after, on the path leading upwards, Garrigue saw lights flickering, faint shadows moving. Under the chapel porch there were footsteps, voices whispering:

'Good evening, Master Arnoton!'

'Good evening, good evening, friends!'

When everyone had entered, my vine-grower, who was very brave, approached softly, looked through the broken door, and saw a strange sight. All these people he had seen passing were ranged in rows around the chancel, in the ruined nave, as if the ancient benches were still there. Beautiful ladies in brocade with coifs of lace, handsome noblemen bedecked from head to foot, peasants in flowered jackets such as our grandfathers wore; everything appeared faded, dusty, old and tired. From time to time night birds, the residents now of the chapel, woken by all the lights, came swooping around the candles whose flames burned erect yet nebulous, as if hidden behind a thin veil. And what amused Garrigue greatly was a certain person wearing large steel spectacles who kept shaking his tall black wig on which one of these birds stood, entangled, silently flapping its wings...

At the far end, a little old man no taller than a child was kneeling in the centre of the chancel, shaking despairingly a little, tongueless, soundless bell; while a priest clothed in old gold moved back and fro before the altar reciting prayers no word of which could be heard ... It was, most surely, Father Balaguère saying his third Low Mass.

Lettres de Mon Moulin, 1869
(Transl. Frederick Davis, 1978)

Beats to the Bar
Roger Woddis

An Ode in Honour of Opening Time

In praise of Bacchus let the boozers sing,
And celebrate the hour of opening:
   The god of sweet oblivion comes!
   Pace the pavement, bite your thumbs,
     Till unlocked doors swing wide
     And you are safe inside.
   Over the teeth and past the gums
     Let the liquor laughter bring,
     Till the strains of life are gone.
Pour it forth in double measure,
Drinking is the door to pleasure:
   Let it widen,
   Drink to Dryden
Who is puking in the john.

Everyone Needs Glasses

Some are hard of hearing,
Some can hardly spell,
Some whose noses sniff at roses
Have no sense of smell.

Some are weak at speaking,
Some can barely read,
Some lack hair, but seem to share
A universal need:

Everyone needs glasses;
All who take a dram
Are light of heart and quote Descartes:
'I drink, therefore I am.'

Punch – Food and Booze Extra,
July 1985.

'The Dons on the Dais Serene'

Roger Lewis

'He saw the dark wainscot and timber'd roof,
The long tables, and the faces merry and keen;
The College Eight and their trainer dining aloof,
The Dons on the dais serene.'

Newbolt: (1862–1938)
'He Fell among Thieves'

OXFORD, seat of learning, is really a croup of eating. The sanctum of college life isn't, as you'd suppose, the library: it's the Hall; upraised like a tabernacle at the far end of that chamber is High Table. There the dons chomp and swill. By the diurnal consumption of vintage wines and dainty dishes do they seek to prove luxury a necessity; grub and grog fuel abstruse cogitation – and what the dons get bears little resemblance to what the undergraduates get. I once dined at Christ Church. Whilst the mob ate fish-fingers and ice-cream, High Table messmates were served scooped-out whole pineapples filled with berries and cream. How to negotiate the rococo pudding? Its being the kind of thing Carmen Miranda used to wear on her head, I wanted to hop on the trestle and dance clickety-clack clickety-clack amongst the silver plate. I picked at a grape and the whole thing imploded. Was it a test of ingenuity, a donnish decider of Intelligence Quotient? Press the right apricot and the thing would launch down the gullet, as innocent as an oyster?

College beanos are complicated rituals, harder to master than the rendering of classical hendecasyllables (for many dons a snip). Table manners are the way to succeed. To be elected a Fellow, bore the Governing body with an account of recondite research by all means (the successful candidate will know that the Governing Body won't

87

follow a word); what matters is comportment in the canteen. A Junior Fellow won't be getting much money; but he will have Dining Rights. Philanthropists who mend towers and build wings, who endow scholarships and repair organs: they, too, if cheques are big and frequent, are borne aloft to High Table, where bat-wing gowns make every night fancy-dress. The garments double as bibs when, after decades on the port, delirium tremens sets in. Gowns also help to disguise the fact that dons are the least snappy dressers in the professional world; they cunningly tailor for themselves baggy suits with more layers of debris down the lapels than Schliemann found in Troy. Excavate a don's waistcoat and a century of university gormandocracy will be revealed. The wardrobe of a Christ Church Canon really did contain many generations' worth of rotting toast. The falling off of good table manners is the only way you can tell if a don has become senile – dons, especially the young ones, always looking ancient and stooped. When a Nobel laureate comes in for a gaudy night with broccoli in his button-hole, it's time he was phased out and given the academic version of geriatric basket-weaving: chairing the Booker Prize.

Dinner begins before dinner with gallons of sherry. The dons then process to the Hall behind the college's boss. The ceremony being pure medievalism, the boss presides like a baron, banging the gavel and calling for grace – which is sung, on special occasions, by a cherubic choir from a minstrels' gallery ('*Sit nomen Domini benedictum, per Jesum Christum Salvatorem nostrum, Amen*'). At Magdalen the dons troop from the Senior Common Room to the honky-tonk along secret paths and passages over the roof. At Christ Church, arrival at the dais is effected through a trapdoor in the cellarage. Up they come, these kith of Lewis Carroll, like demons in a panto. If I had the money I'd install at Wolfson (my latest retreat: built in the 1960s, granted its Royal Charter in 1981) an engine enabling ingress by steam-balloon. At 7:30 the roof of the Hall, a teak teepee, would open, and in we'd come like gods in a Handel opera. As it is, Wolfson, a product of an egalitarian decade, doesn't have a High Table at all. Dons and students share the same facilities – which is pretty revolutionary for Oxford, where rank and status cause such fuss. At St. Catherine's, another 1960s establishment, apartheid does prevail; the dons sit at a table, very many dozen yards long, in high-backed high-tech swivel chairs, like the ones you see in spaceships.

Jakes are another symbol of segregation. At Oriel I seem to recall marble pissoirs in the SCR. It was a wonder to me that a light-fingered Rhodes Scholar hadn't sneaked in, pinched one, and mailed it back to a Folk Museum in the Orange Free State.

Wolfson has no undergraduates; All Souls, which helped to set up Wolfson by lending Sir Isaiah Berlin as its first President, has only Fellows. I dined there a few years ago with an anthropologist. After the pipe-opening Harvey's Bristol Cream in an eyrie in the Hawksmoor towers, my host pushed open a door to a bathroom. I wondered if this was a short-cut to the Hall, some sort of skinnydipping dumb-waiter. 'Have a pee,' commanded the anthropologist, slamming me in. 'I don't want a pee,' I yelped. 'Never,' came a voice through the panels, 'never, *never* my dear boy, turn down the opportunity for a pee.' I gushed the brass taps and rattled the towel rail in semblance of micturition, and exited to see my host fleeing down the stairs begowned. We entered a candlelit stateroom and the eighteenth century. Silent and mumbling figures were glimpsed in the gloom. Light twinkled from the silver cutlery and polished crystal. If ever Sarastro's kingdom in Mozart's *Die Zauberflöte* is to be found, it will be modelled after All Souls.

We sat at a long table running down the middle of the floor; there being no students, there is no need to bother with an elevated platform – though there *is* one for *real* big-wigs to make use of, like Lord Hailsham (who apparently thwacks people with his walking-sticks). To my right was a judge who'd recently read *Earthly Powers* by Anthony Burgess and who claimed it was all about Somerset Maugham; to my left was a gaunt novelist from India, an expert in Macedonian and Eskimo *vers libre*. The food: *Blanchailles*; *Noisettes d'Agneau Beauharnais*; *Crêpes à la Cévenole*. The booze: Moulin de la Grave 1978 and Château la Reille 1976. The plates, chairs and menus were embossed with black ducks: mallards are the All Souls mascot. Along the table was another All Souls mascot, the tin-miner and Dark Lady of English letters, A.L. Rowse.

Next: dessert. Château Bel-Air 1971; Cockburn 1967; Madeira, Finest Old Bual. These were swigged in a gothick cabin remote from the Hall. The decanters, nestling in a silver ship, were wheeled east to west (following the sun); if a diner tarried too long with the precious cargo, the Junior Fellow, traditionally called Mr. Screw, had to tug the alcoholic showboat away with a niblick. After all that, to another snuggery for coffee and brandy...And so it went on...

All Souls dinners are nomadic so that Fellows can jostle and sit next to many different colleagues on the same night. When I dined at Merton with John Carey, term was over and the Hall closed; we ate in the SCR itself. The night spawned memorable conversation, as though scripts had been handed out beforehand by Evelyn Waugh: 'Why are angels always depicted with feathery wings? Why not scales or membranes?' and 'Does anyone in Common Room tonight collect Bradshaws?' and 'How did one travel from Bristol to Edinburgh on the Sabbath in 1890?' (Change at Kettering).

Railways obsess the donnish mind. Many colleges have elaborate tracks and pulleys to wheel the port about; Magdalen has an inclined plane with a cable-car arrangement. John Carey reckoned that the machines and engines hint at obsessions with order and power; the imperiousness of time-tables is paralleled in the fixed laws about how many times the bottles can circulate and in which direction. Also, and rather more intriguingly, the trains are vehicles of nostalgia, allowing indulgent excursions into the past. John Carey pursued the idea in a lecture I heard him give on John Betjeman. The quondam Poet Laureate's love of trains and Metrolands was a love of the Edwardian age he detained himself in. Dons, likewise, preserve a Golden Age by surrounding themselves with bells and rites, customs and taboos.

All of which are easily routed. In the summer Oxford colleges make money by renting grand buildings to American universities, who use superior purchasing power to buy for their charges time under the dreaming spires. Dons moonlight during the Long Vacation by giving lectures and tutorials to students who, in the normal run of things, would have no chance of getting into Oxford. I myself, impecunious, have taught real dimmos. When Trinity was overrun by burly joggers, tartan panty-hose and Burberry coats recently, and I had Dining Rights there, though the architecture of the Hall remained, the architecture of the feast did not. Linen cloths and candles had been superseded by bare boards and Macdonald's paper-serviette dispensers. The Director of the Summer School was in the habit of standing up, thrusting his paunch at the populace, and jawing like a Wild West sheriff. The students whooped and shouted like apaches. *La Darne de Saumon au Champagne* didn't taste the same, self-service. On one heretical occasion, and presumably Lord Quinton, the President, was hiding in his attic with a blanket over his head, the Hall was commandeered for Talent Nite. One of the students I'd been hired to tutor, a frail Emily Dickinson lookalike, who was offended when I made fun of feminists (wouldn't *you* smirk if you were told, in all seriousness, about an aunt so feministic, she went to Sicily to be a nun), topped the bill playing Chopin on her teeth-brace...

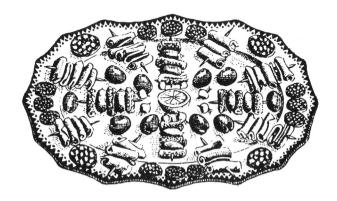

Drinker to Lover, Drunkard to Lecher

Gavin Ewart

A glass of wine
won't say *No*!
or *Don't*! or *Let me go*!
You won't be asked
by any jar:
Who do you think you are?
You'll never hear
from pints of bitter
the hard words of a baby-sitter . . .

No double gin
answers back –
it hasn't got the knack –
it can't look pert,
annoyed or coy –
You're not my kind of boy
is something it
will never answer –
or yet *You're not much of a dancer*!

A vodka's smooth,
can be neat,
and vermouths can be very sweet –
they don't avoid
encroaching lips
or smack your fingertips.
They know their place,
won't fail to meet you,
and know exactly how to treat you!

*The Young Pobble's Guide
to His Toes*, 1984

SOME PEOPLE

Carlo

Portrait of a Maître d'Hôtel

Cyril Ray

HETHER the Café Royal Grill Room is the best restaurant in London I leave to the professional gastronomes to decide, but for me it is the handsomest – red plush and painted ceiling, mirrors and garlanded caryatids, and plenty of light to see them by, all still proclaim the last enchantments of a Golden Age of Dining Out.

Completing the picture is Carlo, the very model of a maître d'hôtel, who has been making me welcome there these twenty years, during which he seems never to have changed – small and slim, elegant at lunchtime in black coat and striped trousers, in the evening in a dinner jacket, and always with a carnation in his buttonhole, where otherwise he could wear the tiny green and red *bottone* of a *cavaliere* of the Italian Order of Merit.

This official recognition signifies the esteem in which London's Italian community holds Carlo Ambrosini, from Piacenza, in northern Italy, a small walled city on the very edge of that renowned knife-and-fork region, Emilia-Romagna. For just as there are chefs' chefs so Carlo is the maître d'hôtels' maître d'hôtel (I prefer that time-honoured title for so time-honoured a holder of it to the American 'maître d'' and the colourless English 'restaurant manager'). Not only in London, either. From Turin's Ristorante Cambio, just like the Grill Room in its more than century-old splendour, to the exquisitely elegant Donatello in San Francisco I have been bidden carry greetings to Carlo from this or that dining-room dignitary whom he had trained. Like Franco, sometime maître d'hôtel at The Hunting Lodge, and now with his own admirable little trattoria, The Cabin, just off Regent Street, they say, 'he taught me all I know.'

Which is what Carlo himself says of Giulio Peduzzi, who presided over the Monseigneur in Jermyn Street, when it was one of London's smartest restaurants, and where Carlo spent a couple of years before the Café Royal. It was under Giulio's eagle eye ('he was very – what d'you call it? – pedantic' says Carlo) that he perfected his already considerable carving skill at slicing smoked salmon into transparent wafers, a joy to watch, and carving duck, at which he is now famous enough to have demonstrated his dexterity on television.

They are all Italians, it will be noticed, and part of Carlo's quality is his Italian feeling for family, so that he behaves as a courteous host, head of a family ('my boys') entertaining honoured guests. This with the natural good manners bred into the heirs of an old civilization – polite, but with none of the po-faced deference of the stage butler, respectful without servility, friendly without familiarity. When I first took my wife to dinner at the Grill Room, I said, 'A very good maître d'hôtel, isn't he?' and she said, 'He's a very nice man, period.'

My son became an admirer of Carlo when he was still a prep-school boy, but observed that he wouldn't like 'having always to be nice, even to people you don't like.' Now that he is grown-up, and knows Carlo better, he recognizes that there is virtually no one that Carlo doesn't like: you would have to try very hard at being beastly to convince Carlo that you weren't entitled to the consideration he regards as the due of every member of the human race.

But what is he like at home? Home is a terraced house in Streatham, where we were invited to Sunday lunch the other day, greeted by Carlo, as dapper in open-necked Tattersall-check shirt and twill trousers as in his workaday dinner-jacket, and served the lunch cooked by Giuliana, as neat and personable and Italianissima as her husband is neat and personable and Italianissimo.

There was ravioli, made by Giuliana with their own eggs, in home-made broth, followed by a home-made *bollito misto* of chicken (home-reared) and beef, with a thick purée of home-grown parsley, with home-grown beans and potatoes. Then a home-reared guinea-fowl, crisply roasted, with stuffed zucchini and a salad, all from the garden, as were the peaches, sliced in wine, and the raspberries and red currants that flavoured the home-made ice-cream. The almond cake was made by Giuliana the way her mother makes it in Piacenza. We drank north-Italian wines and, with our coffee, a *grappa alla ruta*, the potent herb-flavoured colourless grape-skin brandy of northern Italy, made by Giuliana's brother-in-law – in Mitcham.

For happy as Carlo is in what must be one of the most urbane of callings, like many of his fellow-Italians he is a countryman at heart. Everything at that luncheon table was home-grown or home-reared except the beef – and Carlo has known and, as it were, trained his butcher for seventeen years. Apart from butcher's meat, pretty well the only things the Ambrosinis eat at home that they have not produced themselves are what Carlo shoots at weekends with his syndicate in Cambridgeshire and the mushrooms that he and his fellow-Piacentano and maître d'hôtel, Vincenzo Franzini, bring back from the secret places they know about in the nearby woods.

In what most suburban Englishmen would regard simply as a small back-garden in which to grow roses Carlo grows beets and beans and broccoli and at least ten other vegetables; cherries and quinces; apples and pears; persimmons and plums and peaches (more than 200 kilos last year) and figs. My wife enviously counted twelve different herbs, from basil to bergamot, and carried a vast bunch home – this after we had admired the hens (and their eggs), the mallard, the quail and the pigeons.

All is done by Carlo and Giuliana, and when Giuliana is away in Italy to see their new granddaughter (their one daughter is married to a flying-squad policeman in Ferrara) Carlo manages on his own, during his two days off a week and every working-day afternoon, back at Streatham by bus at three, off again to Regent Street by car at five, home again after midnight.

'I'm never bored or sad or not knowing what to do next,' he says, 'Never! I dream about food – not only when I'm asleep, but even when I'm talking to people.' And you realize when he stands by your table in the Grill Room, reciting the fresh vegetables on offer, or explaining this or that sauce, that he knows what he talks about, for he grows such vegetables himself, and knows how they make what in the kitchen.

Happy man!

Gastronomer Royal

Christopher Driver

A NYONE with the money for a meal can express an opinion about a restaurant, for we are all experts on the reactions of our own stomachs. But few writers or talkers have it in them to convey to armchair diners what it is like to spend a couple of hours in this place or that, grand or humble. Restaurants are among the most complex of social institutions. The fleshly pleasures they serve may seem simple, but only a rare emulsion of innocence and experience can do justice to food, drink, setting, staff and clientele, and still give a lively account of the daily performance that brings all these elements together.

The restaurant criticism of Lt.-Col. Nathaniel Newnham-Davis (1854–1917, sometime of the Buffs) a Tory of liberal temper who retired from the Army to the exercise ground that stretches from Pall Mall to Fleet Street, appeared in various books between 1899 and 1914, collected from his contributions to the *Sporting Times*, the *Pall Mall Gazette* and other journals. The *Good Food Guide*, written and edited by Raymond Postgate, a Labour historian, scholar and novelist, first appeared in 1951 after some seminal articles in the *Leader*. Between these dates no London restaurant critic emerged with anything like the style or the influence of these two men. They never met, though it would have been just possible for Newnham-Davis, who died in 1917, to have snorted at the news that Professor J.P.Postgate's bolshie son at Oxford had conscientiously objected to military service.

I owe much information about Newnham-Davis to Postgate's own carefully researched essay on his predecessor that appeared in *The Compleat Imbiber* No. 4 (1961). But long before Raymond left me the editorship of the *Good Food Guide*, with all its dangers and delights, a copy of the colonel's 1899 *Dinners and Diners* had come my way, and worked its spell. To an ill-paid young reporter in ill-fed Liverpool it was perfect escapist reading.

Postgate's part-time but intense preoccupation with restaurants lasted twenty years, but by 1971 he was dead. He had asked me to sort out his books, among which I found not only Newnham-Davis's *Dinners and Diners* and *The Gourmet's Guide to Europe* but also his last collection, *The Gourmet's Guide to London*, published in 1914. Raymond had tracked this down too late for his *Compleat Imbiber* essay, so I am able to pick up the thread where my friend and predecessor laid it down.

Raymond wrote chiefly of the good-humoured soldier, nicknamed 'The Dwarf of Blood' by his friends in the *Pink 'Un* set:*

'There used to be a regular party at 52 Fleet Street, with the contributors, the editors, their friends, Arthur Roberts the comedian and "girls from the Gaiety and the Avenue." One Friday Bessie Bellwood, the beautiful variety actress, started an impromptu pantomime or charade in which all the men had to take part. She was rehearsing some scene or other when Newnham-Davis appeared and she turned on him with:

"Here comes the major for a minor part! Good lud!"

"We'll have to cast him for the Dwarf of Blood."

"What am I to do?" cried Newnham.

"You have to get under the table," said Bessie, "and come out at intervals, shouting, "I am the Dwarf of Blood. Ha! Ha!"'

The name stuck, and he even used it in French – "Le Nain de Sang" – as a *Pink 'Un* by-line for an article on Paris restaurants. Postgate's comment on the style of this set was that of a social-historian as well as an admirer:

'It was a phenomenon of the day, this circle of exuberant writers, using grotesque names not for concealment but merely out of their exuberance, and of their friendship. At the far other end of the political world "Nunquam", "Whiffley Puncto", "Mong Blong" and "The Bounder" were electrifying the Socialist movement and rather shocking the austere ILP. The *Clarion* men were of course infinitely more important ... than Pitcher, Rooty-Tooty and the Dwarf of Blood: but they had a gaiety and a vocabulary in common.'

For my part, I shall write not of the colonel's set but of his meal-

---

* The *Sporting Times*, like football specials of our own day (to say nothing of the *Financial Times*), was printed on pink paper. Ed.

time milieu, of the dishes he ordered and the wines he drank during those blessed, cursed twenty years that ended in 1914; of the delightful companions with whom he dined and drank; and the distinguished professionals who served them. There are five illustrations in *The Gourmet's Guide to London*: drawings of the Cheshire Cheese and of Monsieur Joseph carving a duck – 'a very splendid exhibition of ornate swordsmanship', and photographs of César Ritz, of Rosa Lewis – 'the most celebrated woman cook that this or probably any other age has produced, the great Mrs Glasse not excepted' – and, inevitably, another photograph inscribed by its subject, *'Au delicat Epicurien, Le Colonel Newnham-Davis, en toute cordiale sympathie, A. Escoffier, Novembre 1913.'*

If Newnham-Davis knew anything of the circumstances in which the Ritz-Escoffier régime at the Savoy came to an end he must have been too discreet, as a friend of all concerned, to tell his readers. I have given elsewhere* my reasons for thinking that another Savoy habitué, Arnold Bennett, knew much, and spilled his knowledge, thinly disguised, into his novel, *Grand Babylon Hotel*. But Bennett was a born journalist. If Ritz and Escoffier had been on the take, the Fleet Street rule of gossip, disclosure and the economical use of material would have compelled Bennett into print sooner or later; Newnham-Davis was a newcomer to the inky trade, and it may have been a sense of military honour that kept him silent.

In any case, the colonel was a kind man. Too kind, perhaps, for my own taste in the matter of restaurants, but it will do no harm to quote at the outset the last page he wrote before the shadows closed in:

'Some of my correspondents have asked me why I only write of places that I can conscientiously praise, and why I do not describe my failures. My answer to this is that it is not fair to condemn any restaurant, however humble it may be, on one trial, and that, when I have been given an indifferent meal anywhere, I never go back again to see whether I shall be as badly treated on a second occasion. I prefer to consign to oblivion the stories I could tell of bad eggs and rank butter and cold potatoes, stringy meat and skeleton fowls.

'It is so much better for one's digestion to think of pleasant things than to brood over horrors.'

The jocose nicknames of Newnham's set are themselves a remin-

---

* The *Guardian*, 28 June 1985.

der that the colonel was not himself so much a raffish Edwardian as a well-brought-up Victorian. His literary models could well have been Mark Lemon's Punch Table and its sketches from Thackeray's *alter ego*, M.A. Titmarsh. He was brought up in a typical Victorian family of eight (a nephew, whom Postgate was able to consult for his essay, became a bishop.) It is interesting to place the colonel's gastronomic generation accurately because of the span of his personal memory, for the London restaurant scene as we know it is little more than a century old. The East Room of the Criterion was opened in 1873, 'one of the first, if not the very first, restaurant-rooms designed and decorated to harmonise with feminine frocks and frills ... In the sixties, restaurants were few and far between, and were mostly places where men dined without their feminine belongings. But all this was changed in the seventies, and the East Room did its full share in persuading men that it added pleasure to a good dinner at a restaurant to be faced by a pretty woman.'

The colonel was witness to the change. As a subaltern, in the early seventies, he paid five shillings for a *diner Parisien* at the Criterion, but by the time he was considered steady enough to be entrusted with a political knight's pretty daughter the price was up to half a guinea for the table d'hôte in the East Room:

Caviare
Potage consommé à la Diane
Filets de sole aux délices
Suprêmes de volaille grillées
Carottes nouvelles à la creme
Laitues braisées en cocotte
Cailles à la Sainte-Alliance
Salade de chicorée frisée
Croûte à la Caume
Soufflé glacé à la mandarine

and he was able to explain that: 'The *caille à la Sainte-Alliance*, in imitation of Brillat-Savarin's *faisan à la Sainte-Alliance*, consisted of a truffle in an ortolan, the ortolan being in the quail. In the *croûte Caume*, the tastes of banana and pine-apple and apricot and kirsch all mingle.'

Monsieur Lefevre, maître d'hotel at the Criterion, – tall, with a thin beard, with strong nervous hands that he clasps and unclasps as he talks' – was also 'a man who brought plenty of brain power to bear on the subject of delicate food'. The flighty society girl earned herself a mild reproach from her host for chattering of charades and cycling clubs throughout the consumption of dishes on which so much intelligence had been lavished and 'over which Monsieur Jeannin, *chef de cuisiniers*, had smiled.' On another occasion, Newnham-Davis took a friend's son from Harrow, his own old school, to dinner at the old Trocadero, and tried in vain to tempt him into an opinion about either the decor or the dinner that went beyond the phrase 'jolly good.' 'The *filets mignon*, from his face, Jones minor seemed to like, but he restrained all his emotions with spartan severity ... he ate three sorbets, and looked as if he could tackle three more, which showed me that the real spirit of the Harrow boy was there somewhere under the glacial surface ...'

The colonel had already told his readers that during his early days at the Savoy Monsieur Ritz was quietly teaching the English with money to spend that 'a good dinner is not of necessity a long dinner, and that a few dishes exquisitely cooked are better than a long catalogue of rich dishes.' Ritz's successor, Monsieur Joseph, albeit born in Birmingham, but of French parents, must have been one of the wittiest and most sensitive Frenchmen in London, totally concentrated upon his profession. At a grand dinner for Sarah Bernhardt and other stage luminaries he did much of the cooking himself at a side-table 'because he wished to show actresses and actors, who constantly appeal to the imagination of their audiences, that there was something also in his art to please the eye and stimulate the imagination.'

It would be easy and it would be wrong to give the impression that Newnham-Davis was interested only in the Ritz and the Carlton, actresses and regimental dinners, caviare and champagne. (Like many old-fashioned diners of his time – and in his time he *was* old-fashioned – he clearly regretted the Edwardian champagne fetish, and drank Bernkasteler Doctor and Lafite '78 whenever his fashionable companions would let him.) Inevitably, as with the over-sold London Frenchmen of our own time, Maître Escoffier's *dodine de canard au Chambertin* or Monsieur Granjon's *turbotin Beaumarchais* at the old Berkeley made the news of the day for readers of the magazines that had the colonel as their restaurant correspondent. But his curiosity, both gastronomic and social-historical, extended far more widely. I do not know where else I would go for a vivid account of what was eaten and what was thought of it in

London's Jewish, Chinese and vegetarian restaurants before 1914, not to mention the supper train to Southend and the dining-room of the House of Commons during the winding-up speeches on the Marconi debate in 1912. (They still had the Cockburn 1847 – at a guinea.)

Still less could I find another writer with the same specialized knowledge whose interest in people enlivens his articles with notes on the trends of the time, notably the mighty engine of emancipation that sat young ladies down to tables without chaperons and made Rosa Lewis's all-female kitchen at the Cavendish conceivable.

The Italian invasion of Soho and the west-central districts was exemplified in what we might now call the restaurant-complex that the Italian-Swiss Gatti family made of the old Adelaide Gallery south of the Strand. Newnham-Davis first visited the Adelaide Gallery Gatti's as a schoolboy: 'I ate on that occasion chops and tomato sauce, went on to pastry, and finished with a Welsh rarebit [sic, ed.,] – a schoolboy has no fear of indigestion.' Gatti's, unlike the old chop-houses, possessed another schoolboy's trump card – chips, then 'a novelty in London ... the great Lord Salisbury had a fondness for a chop and chips, and used to gratify it by going to the Adelaide Gallery.' Newnham-Davis returned to Gatti's in the 1880s, 'when I was quartered at Canterbury and at Shorncliffe for a spell of home service.' On a captain's pay, plus a small allowance, 'I know that I received excellent value for money, and the ladies to whom I used to give dinners said that they liked Asti Spumante and Sparkling Hock just as well as champagne – and perhaps they really did, bless them.'

By 1914, a third generation of Gattis was in charge, and the menu had gone far beyond chops and chips – though 'the kitchen of the Adelaide Gallery is one of the few in London that possess a large open fire for roasting, and its Old English cookery is, therefore, always good.' But it was already in the colonel's time difficult to direct a foreign visitor in London to a typical British dinner, well cooked. True, Simpson's was one of the very few places that survived from his book into Postgate's and beyond. (The standards exacted then and now are another matter.) At the Blue Posts in Cork Street – and even there the head waiter was a German veteran of the Franco-Prussian War – 'the steaks, which were a great stand-by of the house, were cut from the mass of beef just in time to be transferred at once to the grill, thus making sure that none of the juices should drain away.'

But Gatti's menu as a whole was already, by the 1900s, what we used to call 'continental', with *carbonnade de boeuf à la Berlinoise*, 1s 2d: *pieds de porc*; *tête de veau*; chump chop *d'agneau*, *purée Bruxellois*, 1s 6d; and a five-shilling table d'hôte that included oyster soup, turbotin, fried eels and casseroled pheasant. Moreover, the wine list was one of the best in London at the price, and as a result of prescient purchases during the slump of 1870/1, 'there is some old cognac in the cellars to which I take off my hat whenever I am privileged to meet it.'

As a turn-of-the-century soldier more familiar with troopships than with Stepney, Newnham-Davis brought more prior knowledge to the Cathay Chinese restaurant in Piccadilly Circus than he did to his dinner at Goldstein's kosher restaurant in the city. 'During the five years that I was quartered in Penang, Singapore and Hong Kong I learned by experience which were the dishes that one could safely eat and which were the delicacies that it was wise to drop under the table. A Chinaman, when he wishes to be very polite, takes up with his chop-sticks some especially dainty morsel from his own plate and pops it into the mouth of his European neighbour. A kindly young man once thus put into my mouth a slip of cold pig's liver wrapped around a prune, and I do not think I ever tasted any nastier combination.'

A Cantonese banker, entertaining the colonel to dinner at his home, converted him, though to 'what I thought quite the most tender and the fattest rabbit I had ever tasted – really a Cantonese edible puppy, fattened on milk and rice.' At Goldstein's menu, on the other hand, 'I groaned aloud. Was it possible, I thought, that any human being could eat a meal of such a length and yet live?' Newnham-Davis had asked not only to taste the solomon gundy, the frimsell, the brown stewed carp (did the ingredients really include treacle and gingerbread?), the roast veal, the smoked beef, the salt tongue, the pickled cucumber and the kugel and apple staffen but also to be shown the ritual practices of this restaurant 'patronized by the "froom", the strictest observers of the Jewish community.'

'Before the *hors d'oeuvre* were brought in, the master of the ceremonies, taking a book from the top of one of the dwarf cupboards, showed me the Grace before meat, a solemn little prayer which is really beautiful in its simplicity. With the Grace comes the ceremony of the host breaking bread, dipping the broken pieces in salt, and handing them round to his guests, who sit with covered heads.'

*　　　*　　　*　　　*

As for *The Gourmet's Guide to Europe*, published by Grant Richards in 1903, Postgate doubted the very existence of the collaborator named on the title page, partly because he was suspicious of the name 'Algernon Bastard' and all the more so because the name is not otherwise known to the British Museum catalogue. But I cannot myself believe that journeys and researches on this pan-European scale could have been undertaken and reported unaided. Every restaurant critic needs his eater; and if the frothy young women whom the colonel delighted to entertain at Prince's or the Piccadilly could not decently be pressed into service at the *cafés chantants* of Moscow ('as the guidebooks sagely remark, "Gentlemen had better leave their ladies at the hotel"') surely the Dwarf of Blood must have had plenty of old comrades-in-arms willing to accompany him the length and breadth of Europe, whether pseudonymously or not. The rewards, after all, must have been irresistible: in Paris alone, at the Café de Paris, the spectacle of the '*haute cocotterie*, who patronise the right fork of the room as you enter'; at Maxim's, where 'any gentleman may conduct the band if he wishes to'; or at the Taverne Pousset, where 'I am never happier at supper-time than when I am sitting in the back room picking crayfish out of a wooden bowl where they swim in savoury liquid, pulling them to pieces, and eating them as they were eaten before forks and spoons put fingers out of fashion.'

Alas, all had to end. Europe's curtain fell while the *Gourmet's Guide to London* was being printed and while the colonel may have been at Carlsbad for August, taking the cure, as was his wont, but choosing for the last time between 'the lean Prague ham or the fatter Westphalian .. no man is really a judge of ham until he has argued for a quarter of an hour as to what breed of pig gives the most appetising slice.' For the last time, I say, because he had already been told that he had Bright's disease, and I must revert to Newnham-Davis's obituarist: 'I well remember the day he came from seeing the specialist. We lunched together: he had a plate of eggs, some stewed apple, and a bottle of Evian water. "It will have to be something like

this every day for the future," he said. "This to a man who was called the Gastronomer Royal." '

Postgate, quoting this, went on, 'When the war came he pulled
every string he could get hold of, and got back in the Army: but even
he could not persuade the doctors to let him go to France. He was
put in charge of the Germans interned in Alexandra Palace: they
were mostly chefs and waiters, and his friends at once declared that
it was a monstrous wangle, to enable him to feed in the greatest luxury. The joke was a wry one: he could eat almost nothing ... he died
in the spring of 1917.'

In similar circumstances, some time in 1970, I suppose, I
remember lunching with Raymond after his own future diet had
been spelled out to him. Later, I was touched to find that he had pin-
ned up in his library the elegiac couplets I had composed for the
melancholy occasion. As a prayer they failed, but as an epitaph they
perhaps express some of the feelings that both these passionate
enjoyers of restaurant life inspired in anyone who shared their
tastes:

> *Heu nimium cupidi ventris tolerata voluptas*
> *Heu nimis incauta pocula rapta manu.*
> *Nunc tibi grex omnis suspendit vota Luculli,*
> *Sollicitusque precor: quot bibis, usque bibas.*

How to Succeed at the Bar

Cyril Ray

A YOUNG member of the Ray family is engaged in research on early twentieth-century politics, and the house is fetlock-deep in books on Haldane—whom I had always regarded as worthy, and dignified in adversity, but hardly a romantic figure, much less a *bon vivant* (though I was to learn that he was renowned for his cellar and his cigars). But perpend...

In about 1882, when Haldane was twenty-five or so, and had made £300 10s. in his three years at the bar, he was at a house-party given by rich Scottish neighbours. An elderly fellow-guest (with, it is recorded, gold-rimmed spectacles) found the young man so understandingly sympathetic to a whispered complaint about the absence of champagne from the dinner-table that he invited him to dine when they were both back in London.

The elderly gentleman was a solicitor—influential, rich, and especially proud of the clarets that, as was then the custom, he could offer his guests after dinner. So, on the appointed evening, out came the Margaux 1864 (already, and to this day, a legendary year), which the company coped with, and then the Lafite 1858. The other guests were of the host's generation and (I quote Dudley Sommer's *Haldane of Cloan*, from which I lift the whole story) 'in various stages of gout and rheumatism...and the host himself by his doctor's orders had been peremptorily cut off.' The Lafite was too much for them and 'Haldane saw that there was nothing else for it...so he proceeded to drink off the bottle, paying a well-deserved tribute to the merits of every glass...walked home none the worse, and with the feeling that he had done a kindly deed.'

A couple of days later, a young man at the door of his attic chambers introduced himself as the son of that night's host, who had said, 'With such a one our firm ought to associate itself, for I am certain that his gifts will raise him to the highest eminence in his profession,' at the same time handing to the future Lord Chancellor his first sizeable brief.

Punch, 23 February 1983

Have It Your Way

Elizabeth David

LWAYS do as you please, and send everybody to Hell, and take the consequences. Damned good Rule of Life.N.' I think we must both have been more than a little tipsy the evening Norman wrote those words on the back page of my copy of *Old Calabria*. They are in a pencilled untidy scrawl that is very different from the neat pen-and-ink inscription, dated 21 May 1940, on the flyleaf of the book, and from the methodical list of 'misprints etc.' written on the title page when he gave me the book. 'Old-fashioned stuff, my dear. Heavy going. I don't know whether you'll be able to get through it.'

I have forgotten the occasion that gave rise to Norman's ferociously worded advice, although I fancy the message was written after a dinner during which he had tried to jolt me out of an entanglement which, as he could see without being told, had already become a burden to me. And the gentleman concerned was not very much to his liking.

'You are leaving with him because you think it is your duty. Duty? Ha! Stay here with me. Let him make do without you.'

'I can't, Norman. I have to go.'

'Have it your way, my dear, have it your way.'

Had I listened to Norman's advice I should have been saved a deal of trouble. Also, I should not, perhaps, have seen Greece and the islands, not spent the war years working in Alexandria and Cairo, not have married and gone to India, not have returned to England, not become involved in the painful business of learning to write about food and cookery. And I should not now be writing this long-overdue tribute to Norman Douglas. Was he right? Was he wrong? Does it matter? I did what I pleased at the time. I took the consequences. That is all that Norman would have wanted to know.

When I met him first, Norman Douglas was seventy-two. I was twenty-four. It was that period in Norman's life when, exiled from his home in Florence and from his possessions, he was living in far-from-prosperous circumstances in a room in the Place Macé in Antibes.

Quite often we met for drinks or a meal together in one or another of the cafés or restaurants of the old lower town, a rather seedy place in those days. There was little evidence of that bacchanal existence that legend attributes to all Riviera resorts.

The establishment Norman chose when he fancied a pasta meal was in a narrow street near the old port. 'We'll meet at George's and have a drink. Then we'll go and tell them we're coming for lunch. No sense in letting them know sooner. If we do, they'll boil the macaroni in advance. Then all we shall get is heated-up muck. Worthless, my dear. We'll give them just twenty minutes. Mind you meet me on the dot.'

At the restaurant he would produce from his pocket a hunk of Parmesan cheese. 'Ask Pascal to be so good as to grate this at our table. Poor stuff, my dear, that Gruyère they give you in France. Useless for macaroni.' And a bunch of fresh basil for the sauce. 'Tear the leaves, mind. Don't chop them. Spoils the flavour.'

Now and again Norman would waylay me as I was buying provisions in the market. 'Let's get out of this hole. Leave that basket at George's. We'll take the bus up toward Vence and go for a little stroll.'

The prospect of a day in Norman's company was exhilarating; that little stroll rather less so. A feeble and unwilling walker, then as now, I found it arduous work trying to keep up with Norman. The way he went stumping up and down those steep and stony paths, myself shambling behind, reversed our ages. And well he knew it.

'Had enough?'

'Nearly.'

'Can you tackle another half kilometre?'

'Why can't we stop here?'

'*Pazienza*. You'll see.'

'I hope so.'

At that time I had not yet come to understand that in every step Norman took there was a perfectly sound purpose, and so was innocently impressed when at the end of that half kilometre, out in the scrub, at the back of beyond, there was a café. One of those two-chair, one-table, one-woman-and-a-dog establishments. Blessed scruffy café. Blessed crumbling crone and mangy dog.

'Can we deal with a litre?'

'Yes, and I'm hungry too.'

'Ha! You won't get much out of *her*. Nothing but bread and that beastly ham. Miserable insipid stuff.' From out of his pocket came a hunk of salami and a clasp knife.

'Do you always carry your own provisions in your pocket?'

'Ha! I should say so. I should advise you to adopt the same rule. Otherwise you may have to put up with what you get. No telling what it may be, nowadays.'

Certain famous passages in Norman Douglas's work, among them Count Caloveglia's dissertation in *South Wind* on the qualities necessary to a good cook, in *Siren Land* the explosive denunciation of Neapolitan fish soup, in *Alone* the passage in which he describes the authentic pre-1914 macaroni, 'those macaroni of a lily-like candour' (enviable phrase – who else could have written it?), have led many people to believe that Norman Douglas was a great epicure in matters gastronomical, and so he was – in an uncommon way; in a way few mortals can ever hope to become. His way was most certainly not the way of the solemn wine-sipper or of the grave debater of recipes. Connoisseurship of this particular kind he left to others. He himself preferred the study of the original sources of his food and wine. Authenticity in these matters was of the first importance to him. (Of this, plenty of evidence can be found by those who care to look into *Old Calabria*, *Together*, *Siren Land*, *Alone*, and *Late Harvest*.) Cause and effect were eminently his concerns, and in their application he taught me some unforgettable lessons.

Once during that last summer of his life, on Capri (he was then eighty-three), I took him a basket of figs from the market in the piazza. He asked me from which stall I had bought them. 'That one down nearest to the steps.'

'Not bad, my dear, not bad. Next time, you could try Graziella. I fancy you'll find her figs are sweeter; just wait a few days, if you can.'

He knew, who better, from which garden those figs came; he was familiar with the history of the trees, he knew their age and in what type of soil they grew; he knew by which tempests, blights, invasions, and plagues that particular property had or had not been affected during the past three hundred years; how many times it had changed hands, in what lawsuits the owners had been involved; that the son now grown up was a man less grasping than his neighbours and was consequently in less of a hurry to pick and sell his fruit before it ripened...I may add that it was not Norman's way to give lectures. These pieces of information emerged gradually, in the course of walks, sessions at the tavern, apropos a chance remark. It was up to you to put two and two together if you were sufficiently interested.

Knowing, as he made it his business wherever he lived and travelled to know, every innkeeper and restaurant owner on the island (including, naturally, Miss Gracie Fields; these two remarkable human beings were much to each other's taste) and all their families and their staff as well, still Norman would rarely go to eat in any establishment without first, in the morning, having looked in; or if he felt too poorly in those latter days, sent a message. What was to be had that day? What fish had come in? Was the mozzarella cheese dripping, positively dripping fresh? Otherwise we should have to have it fried. 'Giovanni's wine will slip down all right, my dear. At least he doesn't pick his grapes green.' When things did not go according to plan – and on Capri this could happen even to Norman Douglas – he wasted no time in recriminations. 'Come on. Nothing to be gained by staying here. Can you deal with a little glass up at the Cercola? Off we go then.'

Well-meaning people nowadays are always telling us to complain when we get a bad meal, to send back a dish if it is not as it should be. I remember, one bleak February day in 1962, reading that a British Cabinet Minister had told the hotel-keepers and caterers assembled at Olympia for the opening of the bi-annual exhibition of icing-sugar buses and models of Windsor Forest in chocolate-work, 'If the food you have in a restaurant is lousy, condemn it...'

At the time Norman Douglas was much in my mind, for it was round about the tenth anniversary of his death. How would he have reacted to this piece of advice? The inelegance of the phrase would not have been to his taste, of that much one can be certain. And from the Shades I think I hear a snort, that snort he gave when he caught you out in a piece of woolly thinking. 'Condemn it? Ha! That won't get you far. Better see you don't have cause for complaint, I'd say. No sense in growling when it's too late.'

Gourmet, February 1969

111

A PHILIPPE
DE ROTHSCHILD
DIPTYCH

I. Mouton, 1918

'My Idea of Paradise'
Philippe de Rothschild

WHEN I was twelve the world went wild, one of those periodic attacks of madness to which the human race is prone. They were having their war and everybody seemed to be enjoying it, in their own peculiar way, with military bands playing, soldiers marching, flags everywhere and tears. Everybody was busy. Papa's car factory was being turned over to ambulances, Mamma was being fitted for a nurse's uniform, Miss May was knitting long khaki socks and crying over the Belgian children. What about this child? Me. 'Oh, the Rothschild boy? He has everything.' I was nobody's darling. There was Mademoiselle Yvonne Grémy, who taught me the violin when I was eight. As I gave my rendering of 'The Meditation' from *Thaïs* and she placed her slender hand on mine to correct the fingering, I nearly fainted. I was madly in love with her but she didn't fancy me at all. In fact she abandoned me, said my musical potential was nil. No, the only living creature who adored me was my pony, Twister, and she was far away.

School was dull but home was worse. Everybody was so busy joining up and dreaming of *La Gloire* that there was nobody left to make us a hot meal. Papa was shut up night and day in his lab at L'Abbaye des Vaulx de Cernay. Even so he managed to write a play, this one about jealousy, a man's suspicion that his ten-year-old child is not his. It was performed at the Marigny and dedicated to a young actress called Juliette.

Mamma, looking very chic in her dark blue and white uniform, was busy with her nurse's training course and Papa suddenly appeared in khaki with red velvet flashes on the collar. Now at the age of forty-two he was a practising doctor for the first time.

Shut away in his lab he had invented a new treatment for burns and designed an ambulance which could make use of the treatment in the front line. Mamma studied the technique and went to the front with the burns unit.

Papa at once wrote another play: *La Femme d'aujourd'hui* ('The Woman of Today').

My father was very bright when he had to face reality. He invented air-tight tubes to preserve the soldier's jam and meat paste. They were like the toothpaste tubes which came much later. He might have been happier if he'd been born a poor man and had to work for his living. As it was he didn't get any credit for his good work. My mother was awarded the Croix de Guerre for hers, but then of course she was prettier.

On my way home from school I kept a sharp lookout for doves and fishes. Doves were the first planes the Germans sent over, mainly to scare us; they were so light they could only carry a few small bombs and the pilot had to open the door, select one and drop it carefully on to the target. Zeppelins were those beautiful silver fish of the sky which had appeared over Paris once or twice, on reconnaissance, bringing everybody out on the streets, more amazed than frightened. I, for one, refused to go to a shelter. I didn't want to miss anything.

In 1918 the Germans were only forty-four miles away and threatening to wipe Paris off the face of the earth. 'Not one stone will be left standing on the other,' said the Kaiser's aide-de-camp, 'then perhaps they will make peace.' The shells from Big Bertha, the Kaiser's mightiest pea-shooter, began to fall on Paris. One landed on the church of St Gervais, when all the people were at mass; very few survived. Another landed on our school. We had all been sent down to the cellars when the shelling started, so we had to escape by the ventilation shaft. It was then that my parents decided to pack me off to Bordeaux. Big Bertha changed the course of my life, the first female to do so.

And Bordeaux? More school, the Lycée Montaigne. At first the name meant nothing to me, Michel Eyquem de Montaigne, merchant, 1533–92, mother of Spanish-Jewish origin, sometime mayor of Bordeaux and a pupil of George Buchanan, who also tutored Mary Queen of Scots' erudite son, James I of England. I began to read his essays and I was held, delighted. I found the lines which had inspired Shakespeare, Marlowe and Webster, and when I learnt that he had retired to his château at the age of thirty-five to write, and declared himself unsuited to marriage and paternity, I decided that was for me. As you have guessed, I was beginning to fancy myself as a solitary dreamer and even scribbling doggerel verses in the corner of my exercise book.

Of course I visited Labrède and sat in Montesquieu's study.

Souvent on a dit gravement des choses puériles,
Souvent on a dit, en badinant, des verités.

I decided to escape from the misery of school into books, so I closed the door on the gloomy apartment in the Rue du Jardin Public and browsed. Sometimes my room became a proper Disneyland. A family of grey mice would appear and play round the table. I made a maze with white flour to amuse them. It got me into terrible trouble with the eagle-eyed Miss May, who was still mounting guard over me.

I wasn't doing so well at the Lycée. I knew nobody and the rigmarole was quite different from my Paris school. Monsieur René Salomé, tutor, arrived, sent from Paris to chivvy me along. What a bore. I had to think up some cunning tricks to give my two watchdogs the slip, but once out of the house I'd race down the road to the docks, the liveliest place in Bordeaux, especially when the American fleet was in. I watched the doughboys unloading their ships and tried my English on them. They were tickled pink.

My side of the family has always prided itself on its English connection and I'd been taught English since babyhood.

I asked if I could drive one of the cranes. They let me. I stayed all day. After a while they let me join in their ball game. We laughed a lot, then they had to leave for the war, and the place would seem very desolate until, inevitably, the next batch arrived to be packed off to the slaughter.

One empty week-end – and week-ends at Bordeaux could be very empty – I thought I might take a look at my grandmother's property, Mouton, near Pauillac, some sixty kilometres away. It was somewhere to go, at least.

The train journey wasn't very inspiring, the countryside looked empty and so flat. There were tumbledown buildings here and there and a few new châteaux with old turrets; but where were the deer parks, the gushing streams stocked with salmon, romantic ruins reflected in artifical lakes? This was very different from the world I knew. As we rumbled along, stopping at every hut, I began to notice the vines. I hadn't recognised them, those endless straight lines of wire and stave supporting the trimmed branches. What workmanship. How did they manage such perfect alignment?

We passed a small Romanesque church. It looked good: sandstone, simple lines. There were glimpses of the broad river Gironde, it gave a touch of life to the scene.

Beyond Pauillac I kept a look-out for this place Mouton. Where was it? What would it be like? There were vines, vines everywhere and a straggling street bordered with hen runs.

Where was the big house? The pediment of a huge stable dominated the scene, and beside it a group of smiling characters stood waiting for someone. Could it be me? There was a grave old man in a wide floppy hat, who turned out to be my grandmother's representative, the Baron de Miollis; Gustave Bonnefous, *maître de chai*, obviously a personage...a stocky chap with big moustaches; Émile Gerbaud, barrel-maker; and a small group of horny-handed blokes in thin blue suits. What are they wearing on their feet? Wooden clogs, *sabots*. There was a bright-eyed boy, Roger Ardouin, and Merilda the cook, a tall, very beautiful woman who stood apart, holding her little daughter, Odette, by the hand.

'Welcome, young Monsieur,' said the old Baron.

The others gave their berets a tug.

'You'll be hungry, Master Philippe,' said Merilda. 'I've made you some cabbage soup and a noodle cake. Odette has put a warm brick in your bed. Say bonjour, child.'

But the little girl was too shy to utter a word. We turned to enter a farmyard. The smell of dung and urine would have knocked you down. Merilda turned aside. 'You've brought out a bottle of the best, Monsieur Bonnefous?'

'Do you like fishing? Can you catch frogs?' It was the boy, Roger. I found it difficult to understand what any of them said. Such a strange accent, swinging and tangy, and such friendliness from people who'd never set eyes on me before.

And the food! I'd never been allowed to taste onions or garlic and I'd never heard of cabbage soup. It landed on the table in an enormous tureen, steaming hot, gales of garlic filled the room when Merilda lifted the lid. Then there was sea-bass stuffed with herbs and roast beef garnished with ceps, freshly gathered in the near-by woods of Béhérré.

That night I drank wine for the first time in my life. At home it was forbidden; my father drank Évian water. I might be given a few drops to colour the water on special occasions, but there was no taste in that. Red beef and wine which smelt like violets. I was drunk. 'In the morning you visit the *chai*.' The way the word was pronounced I though it was some holy temple. These dark strangers might worship anything. I discovered later it was their wine and their women, in that order.

After breakfast I was conducted across the reeking farmyard. Ducking the clothes lines hung with long johns, ladies' drawers and petticoats, we came to an ancient stone shed, the *chai*. Inside it was as cool as a cave, barrels lay in rows on their sides. Monsieur Bonnefous tapped one for me.

'Taste it,' he said.

Three or four of them watched me.

'Savour it...Spit it out. On the floor, where else? You won't spoil the carpet.'

They all laughed. I looked – the floor was of beaten earth. What a change after the terrible chic of my home.

The boy Roger showed me how to harness a horse and spear frogs. I killed enough to make us a feast. He asked me if I was a good shot.

'Of course,' I said. 'What is there to shoot?'

'Only thrushes,' he said, then led me over to the vineyards and started banging away. It is a practice which I have forbidden in my old age, but I have to confess I enjoyed it then, and a fat lot of notice the local youth take of me now.

Most of all I enjoyed getting dirty, trampling through mud, coming back with filthy hands and no one waiting to scold me. It was my idea of paradise.

Milady Vine, 1984

II. The Napa Valley, 1980

Entente Cordiale
Cyril Ray

I began in Honolulu. In 1970, Robert Mondavi was there at the annual convention of the U.S. Wine and Spirit Wholesalers' Association; Philippe de Rothschild was there breaking his journey back to Paris after taking his wife, Pauline, to Auckland, New Zealand, for open-heart surgery (she died in 1976) and, on the way, to meet Philippe Cottin, his *régisseur* – general manager is putting it modestly – of La Baronnie, the great complex of Baron Philippe's interests in the claret country.

Whether they had met before I am not sure – I am pretty certain not – but they already knew a great deal about each other, not only because of the eminence of each in the world of wine, in which they were both discussed and argued over more than most, and because of their respective visits to each other's wine-growing region. More than anything because on frequent visits to the United States Philippe had stayed, sometimes in San Francisco, sometimes in Santa Barbara, with Harry Serlis, for ten years president of the Wine Institute, before that of the Shenley drinks empire, and owner of a cellar of fine wines, among them some of California's most distinguished, which he used to show with pride to his friend from Mouton.

Eventually, Baron Philippe (who had once been widely quoted as saying that 'all California Cabernet Sauvignons taste the same') began to show great interest, and especially in the Cabernet Sauvignons – so much so that he hinted, in only the most general terms, at some sort of contact between Mouton and a California house: Serlis mentioned three or four eminent producers and showed their wines, but recommended Mondavi in particular. He may well have been influenced not only by the quality of the wines already being produced in the late 1960s by the new Robert Mondavi Winery, but by the driving perfectionism in the two men, the larger-than-life dynamism. They would clash, or they would get on like a house on fire: either way, sparks would fly...

Thus it was that one day in 1970, in his hotel in Honolulu, Bob* picked up the telephone to be asked by Philippe Cottin, 'Bob, would you mind coming over to visit the Baron?'

Bob still tells the tale with a schoolboy's excitement: 'I said, "The Baron! My God, what an honour to go and visit the Baron!"'

Americans are impressed by foreign titles, and any wine-grower would, and should, be in awe of Philippe's fame: Bob makes no secret of his feeling like a dog-catcher summoned to the White House, but 'you know how he is – he's like an old shoe; you know – you've got to meet him right off the bat. You know – he puts you completely at ease...'

Philippe expressed an interest in California Cabernet Sauvignons: he wondered if there were some way of his being involved.

'What d'you have in mind?'

'Bob, I don't know – do *you* have any ideas?'

'It was the first I'd ever heard of it,' Bob said to me, more than a dozen years later. 'I had to say that *I* didn't have any ideas, either. We talked for an hour or very nearly, but it ended simply with the Baron saying, "Bob, if you can think of anything, you write and let me know, and if I think of anything I'll do the same."'

Years passed. It may be that Bob, although put so completely at ease in Honolulu, felt that he ought to leave it to Philippe – his senior in rank (for what that is worth, but it may have been unconsciously a factor) and certainly in age, in experience and indeed in reputation – to make the first move. In any case, he had much on his mind, with the rapid expansion of his new winery, his endless experiment and constant travel.

Philippe, meanwhile, had suffered Pauline's long-drawn out illness, worldwide search for cure and eventual untimely death, and had thrown himself wholeheartedly into developing still further his

---

* From this point, in this chapter at any rate, they will be 'Bob' and 'Philippe', for I tell the story as they each told it to me, and it seems stilted, as I write, to be setting down the surname of the one and the title of the other – though Bob still refers to Philippe as 'the Baron'.

Bordeaux interests – the change of name of his holding firm in Pauillac, from La Bergerie to La Baronnie, was no mere window-dressing: it signified an extension of frontiers.

Here, perhaps, was another frontier across which to march – anyway, it was in August 1978, eight years after the Honolulu meeting, that Philippe's agent in Santa Barbara telephoned: 'D'you remember, the Baron talked to you about a joint venture in California? Is there any way you could get together?'

That November, Bob and his daughter Marcia flew to Paris to be glided away by limousine to the Médoc and have their luggage carried by deferential chambermaids into Grand Mouton, the transmogrified stable-block, now luxurious house, library and exquisite museum, opposite what was the little nineteenth-century château. It was hard to decide, five years later, when Bob still bubbled over, in a voice like iron-tyred wheels on a gravel path, what had impressed him most – the limousine, the chambermaids, or that Philippe greeted him with 'Hiya, Bob!'

Bob still remembers the *vin blanc cassis* served before dinner that night, made with *cassis* from Philippe's own blackcurrants; with the quails, a bottle of Mouton over which he teased his host with having used the same cask for the *cassis* and the claret – not the first nor the last talented taster to mention blackcurrants in a consideration of Mouton – another Mouton, a hundred years old; and then a glass of Yquem, as I have always known Philippe to serve it – frozen into a near-sorbet with icicles in the glass: 'Don't ever tell Lur Saluces what I do to his wine, or he'll disown me!' As though he cared two hoots, or even a hoot and a half, for what anyone, marquis or milkman, thought about Philippe de Rothschild and how he liked to take his wine...

No business talk at dinner, but when the maid came to take orders for breakfast ('What a beautiful breakfast! Hadn't had breakfast in bed for twenty-five years – not since I was in hospital!') he was asked would he mind meeting Philippe in Philippe's bedroom tomorrow at half-past nine – and especially (one can picture Philippe's impish smile) – would Marcia mind? Philippe does all his morning's work – and a day's work is done every morning – in bed, surrounded by telephones and books and files, with a desk across his lap and a golden retriever at the foot of the bed: 'you think better with your legs up than with your legs dangling down.'

And that's the way it was, with Philippe 'looking every bit a baron, but still, you know, like an old shoe – so easy to talk to.' I have never found an old shoe all that easy to talk to, but I knew what Bob meant. 'And, by the way,' said Bob, 'aren't those sheets sensuous? So thin, so fine – just *sensuous!*' Bob had got hold of a fancy new word from somewhere, and wore it like a carnation in a buttonhole.

This time, Bob says, Philippe's mind was made up: he was interested in a joint venture – a Napa Valley wine jointly produced – and the two men talked for two hours outlining a prospective programme; they must each have given the other time to talk, which to me seems almost miraculous. According to Bob, anyway, 'the Baron always asked me my opinion first about each idea he had, before he made it positive.' There were to be five thousand cases of wine for the first year's production; the wine was to bear both names and be jointly owned. There was to be only one wine, a Cabernet Sauvignon, and Philippe said that it should have a name of its own, not just be so-and-so's Cabernet Sauvignon. 'That's if we can think of one,' he added. It was to take a long time...

Bob said that 'if we want to be unique, we should have our own vineyards and our own winery,' and this was agreed, but what in the meantime? Clearly, unless the whole project was to be postponed for years, while vines were planted and began to yield (some three to five years) and a winery was built and equipped (God knew how long) a wine must be made; to get the joint venture off the ground.

This was where Philippe took Bob completely by surprise:

'Since you're the one who's in California, you'd better make the first wine.'

Had he said that the wine would have to be made in California, but by his own people, Bob told me, 'I'd have said, "Baron, it was a wonderful dinner and a wonderful breakfast in bed: thank you very much, and now I'll be on my way." But he's too shrewd, too smart...' What they agreed was that until they could find and make operational their joint-venture vineyards and winery, the grapes would come from Bob's vineyards and the wine be made in Bob's winery, jointly by a team led by Lucien Sionneau from Mouton, and a Mondavi team captained by Bob's son, Tim.

Bob and Philippe each had a board of directors to consult, but I gather that this turned out to be, as expected, a formality. What was more important was the attitude of the wine-making teams – as Philippe Cottin pointed out to Philippe de Rothschild, 'you and Bob may agree, but if Sionneau and Tim don't get on, *no deal.*' And to

Bob, 'I don't think Sionneau's ever been as far from Mouton as Paris: he'll go to California for the Baron, but you'd better know what you're up against...'

Sionneau flew to California. He was shown everything, he tasted everything, visiting other wineries in the Napa Valley and tasting their Cabernet Sauvignons – 125 in all, Bob says. He flew back happy, and was back in California again in three months; he has not a word of English and Tim has little French (usually Philippe Cottin was there, which was a help, but not essential, for they got on, in Bob's words, 'like peas in a pod'). In three years, Sionneau visited Oakville eight times.

Before that, though, as they agreed that eventually the Joint Venture – already its unofficial code name – would have to have its own vineyards, Philippe said, 'Bob, I hear that you've a sizeable acreage in the Napa Valley – would you mind selling twenty or twenty-five acres to the Joint Venture?'

'I looked him square in the eye,' Bob recalls, 'and I said, "would *you* sell twenty-five of *yours*?'

'Oh, *no*...'

'Then *I* won't either...'

Two of a kind.

They decided to give themselves until 31 December 1981 to buy land for the Joint Venture, and Philippe suggested that in the meantime, for the first vintage, Bob would provide the grapes and Philippe the barrels: if the wine was not a success, then Bob would pay for the barrels at cost price, and would keep the wine. Again, two of a kind: it was a gentleman's agreement, and it would never have been broken. It has never needed to be...

It had taken the two men two hours in Philippe's bedroom to decide everything and to know positively that they were going ahead: it took the lawyers nearly two years to get contracts put together – 'everything at the pace of oxen,' commented Philippe; 'each trying to outdo the other,' said Bob, 'and then having to hassle with the bureaucrats to get money out of France and into the States.'

The bedroom meeting was in August 1978; it was on 16 April 1980 that it was announced at press conferences in Paris and San Francisco that an agreement had been signed for a joint venture involving the wine-makers of the Robert Mondavi Winery and of Château Mouton-Rothschild in producing a limited amount of 'premium' wine in the Napa Valley. Other French houses had bought vineyards in the valley, but this was the first alliance on equal – or any other – terms between a great French wine-growing establishment and a great California winery with the object of producing a wine with a personality of its own, neither Mondavi nor Mouton, but a Napa Valley Cabernet Sauvignon, made jointly by two of the most highly skilled, experienced and dedicated wine-making teams in the world of wine. It was a turning-point – perhaps it would be better to say finger-post – in what Edward Hyams has described as the social history of the wine vine.* It is noteworthy that Philippe and Bob, both at the San Francisco conference, were, respectively, just seventy-eight and within a couple of months of being sixty-seven. They seemed no older – in spirit and in far-sightedness, at any rate – than the daughter of the one and the son of the other, Philippine de Rothschild and Michael Mondavi, who raised glasses of the 1970 Mouton and the 1975 Robert Mondavi Cabernet Sauvignon Reserve at the Paris conference, to the future of the Joint Venture.

Land has since been bought for the Joint Venture – fifty acres at first and then another fifty, most of it just across the road from the Mondavi winery, some a few miles to the south-east – after a series of blind tastings of the wines they can produce, with Lucien Sionneau always a member of the tasting panel. After the first fifty acres had been bought, and as things were clearly going so well, Bob did agree to sell forty acres of his own To Kalon vineyards to the Joint Venture, which thus owns 140 acres, belonging not to Mouton or Mondavi but to itself, virtually all planted with Cabernet Sauvignon, but a little Cabernet Franc, the proportions for the blend depending on how each year's vintage balances. The blends for the first four are:

1979	80%	Cabernet Sauvignon
	16%	Cabernet Franc
	4%	Merlot
1980	96%	Cabernet Sauvignon
	4%	Cabernet Franc
1981	93%	Cabernet Sauvignon
	7%	Cabernet Franc
1982	85%	Cabernet Sauvignon
	15%	Cabernet Franc

* The sub-title of his *Dionysus* (1965)

Early spring of 1984 saw the first cautious release on to the general market of 5000 cases of the 1979 and 1980 vintages, in California, New York, Illinois, Florida, Texas, Massachusetts and the District of Columbia, at a recommended retail price of about 50 dollars a bottle. In an interview he gave James Laube of the *Wine Spectator* Bob said that the wine 'has a subtlety to it...it's in harmony. That's due to the fact that we have worked together so close that we've taken advantage of each other's knowledge and skills. The wine has structure and elegance. It's like a human being that has gone to finishing school but is natural at the same time. It's what I call simple elegance in wine to the point where you almost overlook it.'

For once, Philippe was markedly less loquacious than Bob: 'the wine is doing very well, but I am more accustomed to old wines than to young wines.' Bob foresaw difficulties with distributors, 'because the wine won't be something so much to drink as something to keep for history. The occasion will be bigger than the wine...we've been besieged by people who want to taste it and that's why we decided not to let anyone taste it until it's ready to be released.' All that can be said of the two first two vintages is that the 1979 was fermented at 31°C for three to five days, and in contact with the skins for an average of ten (there were minor differences between vats). It spent just over two years in 60-gallon casks of Nevers oak and was racked every three months, as at Mouton. It was exactly the same with the 1980s, save that it spent .3 months longer in oak (24.5 months as against 24.2) and may be a little over the hoped for 13 degrees alcohol – the 1979 was just under.

The point had already been made that these first wines would be regarded as museum pieces. On 21 June 1981, at the first Napa Valley Wine Auction (a charity event) at St Helena, the first case of the 1979 was bought, untasted, by a Syracuse wine-merchant, Charles Mara, for 24,000 dollars – 2000 dollars a bottle – a record price for any American wine; at the same event in 1983 an imperial of the same vintage (a bottle peculiar to Bordeaux containing six litres, eight bottles) was bought for 5200 dollars by John Grisanti, a Tennessee restaurateur, who took delivery early in 1984 to sell it again at auction for the benefit of a Memphis hospital.

*   *   *

Much of what Bob had told me at Oakville Philippe told me to the same effect later, in his rooms in Albany, when my wife out a tape-recorder under his nose, as he lay, as always of a morning, in bed: 'I don't know why: perhaps it's because of keeping my bottom steady' – a remark that still baffles me...

(He recalled that it was in bed that he first received Bob and Marcia: 'Everyone thought I'd be flirtatious with Marcia,' he chuckled delightedly: what he meant was that that was what he hoped everyone thought, or what he intended everyone to think. He cherishes his not undeserved reputation as a lady's man...'but she's very austere, very severe and business-like, even more than her father.')

He said that all he had been afraid of was 'sending all my boys to California: they're peasants, close to the soil, their own soil; their customs; the way they always eat their soup; very traditional. If they come back with long faces, then I can't treat with the Americans; if they come back happy, I sign tomorrow.

'They came back smiling, partly on account of Bob, partly on account of his two sons. There were two generations represented in each team – the old got on with the young and the young got on with the old. So I signed.' There was no question of how the two principals themselves got on. Of Bob, who spoke of him affectionately as an old shoe, Philippe said, 'always ready for a joke and a slap on the shoulder, happy with life and happy with what he's doing.'

The only trouble – and I can claim to have foreseen this, for I said as much when I first heard of the Joint Venture – was never over personalities, never over the wine and how to make it: it was over the name and the label. 'Bob left it to me at first' – the name, that is – 'and then, when I choose one, he doesn't agree.'

It had to indicate the partnership between Mondavi and Mouton without either being given precedence over the other. It had to be a word that both French and American wine-drinkers would understand and could pronounce. The two men – and their advisers – played about with variations on the theme of 'Duo' and 'Duet'; Philippe suggested 'Janus', the two-faced god, for two heads had been put together to make the wine – Bob said that no American had ever heard of him; Bob wanted 'Mondavi-Rothschild', but Philippe did not care for the idea; there was some playing around with the idea of a name based on Oakville, where the wine was made, and oak, in which it matured, but it sounded too much like an undignified 'okey-doke'.

Finally, everyone agreed on 'Alliance', which could not have been better, saying all that needed to be said, and pronounceable in both languages – only to discover that Renault was selling an 'Alliance' car all over the States.

Philippe was keen on 'Opus' – the first of the vintages to be 'Opus One' – and had told me as long before as June 1983, at a party in Albany, that it had been positively decided on, but I could get no confirmation from Oakville, where they maintained that *nothing* had been decided. As it turned out, it had been, but reluctantly. Philippe, who told James Laube of the *Wine Spectator* that 'Opus' was a name that 'fitted both men, both countries, and had a musical flair...a bottle of wine is a symphony to me, a glass of wine is a melody. Because "opus" means a musical composition of great quality, I thought it was a good trademark for our wine.'

Bob told Philippe that no American would know what it meant, but finally gave in, saying to the same reporter, 'I tell you – we went over so many names, hundreds in fact and every time we got a name we liked – for one reason or another – there was a double meaning, either in France or in this country. But it was the Baron's idea we call it "Opus One"* and I went along with him.'

Helped to do so, I learned with delight, by an incident as unrehearsed and unexpected as could be. At the 1983 Summer Jazz Festival on the lawn outside the Vineyard Room of the Mondavi winery, held in June–July, the leader of the Preservation Hall Jazz Band from New Orleans, announcing a next item, said that where, a generation ago, the Mills Brothers had first played it, they said that this was its first ever performance in public, 'So let's call it "Opus One".' He knew nothing of the discussion about the label and the name –

---

* A suprising choice of name. Even more surprising is that someone else had already thought of it for another wine (or 'wine'). The *Wine Spectator* of San Francisco for 1–15 December 1983 reported that 'residents of Brogue, Pennsylvania, have been drinking "Opus 1" for close to a year now. It costs $5.95 a bottle, and can be bought by the case at the local grocery store. The brothers John and Tim Crouch make their Opus 1 from peaches and grapes – the peaches give it a peachy nose and the grapes give the wine a vinous quality.' (Good thing for a wine to have...) The Crouch brothers had their label *approved* by the Bureau of Alcohol, Tobacco and Firearms – which body looks after what the law requires of a label: alcohol content, bottle capacity, name and address of producer, and so on. This does not, however, register or *patent* a name, whereas the United States Trade Mark and Patent Office does, and the Mondavi lawyers registered 'Opus One' there in January 1983.

the latter had been registered in the January of that year but not yet accepted by Bob.

What Bob did not give in over was the label. Philippe, famous for his Mouton labels, a different one every year for nearly forty years, by artists as distinguished as Picasso and Henry Moore, Braque and Chagall, had strong views of his own. One of his ideas was that the word 'Opus', printed fairly boldly on the label should be supported by a musical score, with the word repeated in minuscule lettering as notes upon the staves.

Bob, whose own Mondavi Winery labels are, to my mind, the best in California, must have thought this too egg-headed, and just as he had given way over the name, Philippe gave way over the label. Someone suggested a combination of the Mouton ram with the California bear – the symbol that appeared on the flag of the short-lived Republic of California, which is still the state flag – but the notion was discarded along with literally hundreds of others. After two years of debate and, Philippe told me, after some three or four hundred designs had been submitted, some brought from San Francisco to Mouton by two designers, he reluctantly accepted part of a design by Susan Roach Pate of The Studio, San Francisco – that part showing the faces of the two men, Bob and Philippe, in silhouette, back to back – but he re-designed the rest. I said when I first saw it that I could not believe that the label would last as long as Mallette Dean's dignified wood-engraving for the Mondavi Winery wines, or his modestly elegant monogram for the 'Bob' wines of Woodbridge, or be so much admired and sought after as Mouton's annual surprise for collectors.

However, I understand that in future designs the two-headed silhouette will be replaced, perhaps by a trophy of musical instruments, perhaps by a stylized drawing or engraving of a single instrument – I hope so, for the present label is unworthy of what cannot but be a noble wine...

Robert Mondavi and the Napa Valley, 1984

THREE PLATES
OF PASTA

Pasta? Basta!

Paul Dehn

GRAZIE, *cameriere*! That means 'Thank you, waiter!' in Italian, Simon.

No, old chap. Not that way. Look, let Uncle show you. If little Italian boys can eat spaghetti tidily at the age of six, so can little English ones. Now. Hold your fork in your *right* hand and plunge it vertically into the spaghetti, no, Simon, I said *vert—Cameriere! Dell'acqua calda, per favore, subito!* That's Italian for 'Some hot water, please, quickly.'

Grazie, cameriere.

There. That ought to dry out. You'd better tuck your napkin down your collar and put mine over your trousers. Now, shall we have another go? Plun—I mean put your fork upright into the spaghetti. Good. Now twirl the fork round so that—no, slowly, Simon, *slowly*, not like an egg-whisk. Oh, good grief. *Scusi, Signora. Si. No. No. Si. Cameriere! Dell'acqua calda per la signora alla next* table *e per me un nuovo* napkin.

Grazie, cameriere.

Now don't get discouraged, old chap. Just hang on to your fork. I said hang *on*—oh, Simon. No. Just leave it lying there among the spaghetti. Dammit, Simon, I said *don't* pick it up or you'll get tomato all over your—*CAMERIERE! Un* fingerbowl, *subito.*

Grazie, cameriere.

Now there's nothing to cry about, Simon. It's only a plate of spaghetti and we're going to get it licked, ha, ha, ha.

Better now? Splendid. Just one more go. And please try to listen. Put the fork upright in the spaghetti. Good. Twirl the fork *slowly*, so that you can *collect* the spaghetti *round* it. Very good. Right, you can stop twirling now. Simon, I said STOP twirling, you've collected half a plateful. No, don't *un*twirl or you'll lose the lot, just leave it as it is. Whew.

Now. *Raise* your fork—SLOWLY, Simon—till you've lifted the spaghetti on your *fork* clear of the spaghetti on the *plate*. Go on, lift it. Higher. Higher, Simon. Dammit, if little Italian boys of six can reach, so can little English—all right, stand if you want to. Higher. High—SIMON GET OFF THAT CHAIR OR I'LL BELT THE LIVING—*Cameriere! Ancora dell'acqua calda, per favore, ed un* table-cloth *ed un* bandage *ed un po d'*iodine...

Simon, what the hell are you laughing at? Oh. I see. Well, it may interest you to know that 'po' is the Italian for 'little'.

How about packing it in, old chap, and having something simple like—like soup? Certainly not. In a *plate*. No? One last, final bash at the spaghetti? That's the spirit. Here we go then.

Put your fork upright in what's left on the plate. Good. Twirl slowly. Good. Lift it clear. *Very* good. I say, this is exciting, isn't it? Now put the fork in your mouth and don't bother about the bits hanging out—just suck. Suck, Simon. I beg your pardon? Look, I shouldn't bother to try to speak, old chap, it's almost impossible to under—ah. Well, swallow what's actually *in* your mouth and *then* suck.

Suck, Simon. And again. And again. Six inches. Five inches. Four, three, two, one—BRAVO! You've done it, old chap. Congratulations. Your uncle's proud of you. Like it? Mm. Well, it's bound to be a bit cold and greasy, isn't it, after all the time we took. The thing is to eat it quickly while it's still piping hot but that takes a bit of—Simon, are you all right? Have a drink of water, no don't have a drink of water, try putting your head between your legs. No, Simon, between *your* legs. Grab a napkin. No, not *that* napkin—it's full of— *Cameriere! Subitissimo! Un* basin.

The Punch Guide to Good Living, n.d.
(A *Punch* anthology circa 1973)

'I Like All Simple Things...'

Somerset Maugham

Do you like macaroni?' said R.

'What do you mean by macaroni?' answered Ashenden. 'It is like asking me if I like poetry. I like Keats and Wordsworth and Verlaine and Goethe. When you say macaroni, do you mean *spaghetti, tagliatelli, vermicelli, fettuccini, tufali, farfalli,* or just macaroni?'

'Macaroni,' replied R., a man of few words.

'I like all simple things, boiled eggs, oysters and caviare, *truite au bleu,* grilled salmon, roast lamb (the saddle by preference), cold grouse, treacle tart, and rice pudding. But of all simple things the only one I can eat day in and day out, not only without disgust but with the eagerness of an appetite unimpaired by excess, is macaroni.'

'I am glad of that because I want you to go down to Italy.'

Ashenden had come from Geneva to meet R. at Lyons and having got there before him had spent the afternoon wandering about the dull, busy, and prosaic streets of that thriving city. They were sitting now in a restaurant on the *place* to which Ashenden had taken R. on his arrival because it was reputed to give you the best food in that part of France. But since in so crowded a resort (for the Lyonese like a good dinner) you never knew what inquisitive ears were pricked up to catch any useful piece of information that might fall from your lips, they had contented themselves with talking of indifferent things. They had reached the end of an admirable repast.

'Have another glass of brandy?' said R.

'No, thank you,' answered Ashenden, who was of an abstemious turn.

'One should do what one can to mitigate the rigours of war,' remarked R. as he took the bottle and poured out a glass for himself and another for Ashenden.

Ashenden, thinking it would be affectation to protest, let the gesture pass, but felt bound to remonstrate with his chief on the unseemly manner in which he held the bottle.

'In my youth I was always taught that you should take a woman by the waist and a bottle by the neck,' he murmured.

'I am glad you told me. I shall continue to hold a bottle by the waist and give women a wide berth.'

Ashenden, 1928

How To Do It

Norman Lewis

OU find your duties sufficiently strenuous?'

'I should do so if I allowed them to be. As it is, I arrange for the Council to meet here, and we always conduct our business over a good meal. That makes things easier. Incidentally, the Councillors will be arriving in a few minutes' time and we shall all have dinner together.'

The Councillors were now beginning to arrive, and shortly afterwards they were ushered into an adjoining room where at the invitation of the Sindaco they settled like graceful carrion birds round the dinner table.

The Sindaco assisted his old father into a kind of infant's chair at the head of the table, where he perched, an aged but watchful condor above the glistening wilderness of table-linen and plate.

On a side-table a curious ceremony was being performed. A maid-servant was forking masses of spaghetti from a huge pot and weighing it on a pair of scales before transferring it to the plates.

The Sindaco winked pleasantly at Manning. 'A little game of ours. A harmless competition we get a lot of fun out of, although the results are a foregone conclusion. It's a contest to see who can eat the most spaghetti. Except on rare occasions when he's bilious, Dr. Serra always wins.'

The doctor, a pinkish man with the angry eyes of chronic dyspepsia, shook his head modestly.

The fame of Dr. Serra, the only practising medical man to be present, had already reached Manning's ears. The doctor came of a gifted family of Amalfitano craftsmen who specialized in the fabrication of those ingenious and intricate cabinets of inlaid woods sold chiefly to the tourists of Naples, Sorrento and Capri. The doctor, having inherited all the family's manipulative genius, plus vision in excess of the average, had put this to good use in becoming a surgeon. He specialized in the restoration of virginity by surgical means, openly boasting of having improved upon nature's provisions in this matter by supplying hymens of varying degrees of resistance, according to taste. His fee for this service was 10,000 lire. In this way he had quickly amassed a fortune and acquired a following of regular and highly satisfied clients.

'Papa's the runner up when he competes,' the Sindaco continued, 'although he held his place as champion until only a few years ago. As usual, I'm nowhere in the running. Perhaps competition doesn't accord with my philosophic outlook. Still, I try to be a sportsman and look forward to the day when I may acquit myself with more distinction. It takes the best part of a lifetime to develop a real spaghetti stomach.'

Each Councillor was now confronted with his plate, upon which a mountain of spaghetti rose up, writhing like extruded bowels and ensanguined with tomato sauce.

The Sindaco paused between huge mouthfuls, the tattered remnants of which, hanging tusk-like from his teeth, reminded Manning of an emaciated but amiable boar. 'Look at Papa,' he panted.

The old man, in fact, was cleaning up his plateful with a display of the most impressive technique. Don Arturo's method was to plunge his fork deep into the mound on his plate, and with a few preliminary twists bring up a writhing mass, the load in miniature of a hay-maker. This would be supported by his spoon held beneath until by dint of further skilful twists of the fork the mass impaled on its prongs assumed a compact shape. As this burden neared them, the jaws extended incredibly, obviously to the point of dislocation, in a way indeed which Manning had until now regarded as being the peculiar attribute of certain snakes. The eyes followed the approaching load with an ever-increasing squint. The portals of the mouth reached, Manning heard the faintest hiss, the jaws snapped to, and for a fraction of a second the old man's face was twisted in a grin of passion. Instead, however, of the period of rumination which Manning had expected, a champing of the gums in at least a token of mastication, the cheeks immediately deflated, and this deflation was followed by a sudden boa-constrictor-like distention of the neck, a dangerous heightening of the face's colour, a final convulsion — and already Don Arturo's fork was at work again.

'The ornamental style — supposed to have been introduced by the Bourbons,' said the Sindaco. 'Don Fernando IV was said to have demonstrated it for the first time in his box at the Naples opera. Of course, it is one of those old-world graces, a gastronomic gongorism that still survives here and there but to all intents and purposes is as obsolete as lavender spats or a coach and pair. Spectacular, yes — but for competitive purposes lacking in science and speed. It's like trying to win a swimming race with the breast stroke: you just tire yourself out. Now watch Dr. Serra.'

Even to a layman it was obvious that the doctor outclassed all the rest. Above all, his seriousness, his grim concentration, were in evidence. The doctor was conducting a total war. He was demolishing a strong-point, stabbing at his plate viciously and with tremendous speed, ruthlessly severing with the edge of his fork those coils of spaghetti which Don Arturo had tenderly preserved intact. Whereas Don Arturo's expression had been lascivious, Dr. Serra's was indignant. Don Arturo ravished, he slaughtered. This was the victory of hate over love.

'You are not eating,' protested the Sindaco with concern.

Manning had, in fact, come to the end of his tether after the first few mouthfuls. He felt an intolerable distention of the stomach, although there was no apparent decrease in the mound on his plate.

'Take your time,' said the Sindaco, 'take your time. You will be feeling empty again in a few minutes.' He signalled to the maid to

136

weigh out another plateful. 'To you, of course, spaghetti is something new. Perhaps it takes a little time to get used to it, but let me try to explain to you how a practised eater feels — his philosophy, in fact. To us it provides the perfect alliance between the senses of taste and touch. Half the pleasure comes from the act of swallowing. With other victuals this part of the procedure is unavoidably hasty and unimportant, but we spaghetti eaters succeed in protracting it by swallowing mouthfuls which cram the whole of the gorge. By virtue of its blandness, it cannot cause discomfort, and its passage downwards is controlled at will by the real expert — the *illuminé* — by the development of special muscles. All these things, of course, take time.'

The next few minutes were given over to silent consumption, and then after unsuccessfully pressing further helpings on the guests the Sindaco rose to announce that Dr. Serra had won the competition with an intake of 1.4 kilogrammes. The doctor acknowledged the cheers and hand clapping, with a weary smile. 'I was hoping to have broken my record today. Probably could have done so with the white kind of pasta. No reflection on you, Sindaco, of course. I realize it is next door to impossible to get. In fact, with this accursed black market going on as it is quite unchecked, who knows when we will ever see the real thing again?'

Within the Labyrinth, 1950

Madame Poulard's Secret

Elizabeth David

ONCE upon a time there was a celebrated restaurant called the Hôtel de la Tête d'Or on the Mont-St-Michel just off the coast of Normandy. The reputation of this house was built upon one single menu which was served day in day out for year after year. It consisted of an omelette, ham, a fried sole, *pré-salé* lamb cutlets with potatoes, a roast chicken and salad, and a dessert. Cider and butter were put upon the table and were thrown in with the price of the meal, which was two francs fifty in pre-1914 currency.

But it wasn't so much what now appears to us as the almost absurd lavishness of the menu which made Madame Poulard, proprietress of the hotel, celebrated throughout France. It was the exquisite lightness and beauty of the omelettes, cooked by the proprietress herself, which brought tourists flocking to the *mère* Poulard's table.

Quite a few of these customers subsequently attempted to explain the particular magic which Madame Poulard exercised over her eggs and her frying pan in terms of those culinary secrets which are so dear to the hearts of all who believe that cookery consists of a series of conjuring tricks. She mixed water with the eggs, one writer would say, she added cream asserted another, she had a specially made pan said a third, she reared a breed of hens unknown to the rest of France claimed a fourth. Before long, recipes for the *omelette de la mère Poulard* began to appear in magazines and cookery books. Some of these recipes were very much on the fanciful side. One I have seen even goes so far as to suggest she put *foie gras* into the omelette. Each writer in turn implied that to him or her alone had Madam Poulard confided the secret of her omelettes.

At last, one fine day, a Frenchman called M. Robert .Viel, interested in fact rather than surmise, wrote to Madam Poulard, by this time long retired from her arduous labours, and asked her once and for all to clear up the matter. Her reply, published in 1932 in a magazine called *La Table*, ran as follows:

6 June 1932

Monsieur Viel,

Here is the recipe for the omelette: I break some good eggs in a bowl, I beat them well, I put a good piece of butter in the pan, I throw the eggs into it, and I shake it constantly. I am happy, monsieur, if this recipe pleases you.

Annette Poulard.

An Omelette and a Glass of Wine, 1984

Wine and/or Women

Peter Dickinson

Woman, as every schoolboy knows,
   Assorts but ill with wine.
Her cheek may be the scented rose,
   Her embonpoint divine.
     (Far gone, far gone the diner able
      To see much more—beneath the table.)
But oh, the odour of that rose,
   The heaving of that chest,
Confounds the senses, fills the nose—
   What wine can stand the test?
     I learned this wisdom from my father
      Who told me, nothing loth,
     'Enjoy whichever you would rather
      But don't, my son, try both.'

Love of good wine, each housewife knows,
   Is not so good for love.
How often does some lad propose
   Some lassie's worth to prove
     (Selecting her because the wine
      Has somehow made the wit resign.)
But she, when tempted to his cell
   With maidenly demur,
Finds he who does himself too well
   Does not so well with her.
     I learned this wisdom from my granny:
     'They both are worth the bother,
     But if you'd be a Man, my mannie,
     You must choose one or other.'

Now we, as all assembled know,
    Have made a useful hoard
And rare indeed is the Château
    Or girl, we can't afford.
      But still we face this problem which
      Afflicts the poor man and the rich.
Let us resignedly carouse,
    Forgetting love's delight.
This is the night, my friends, to souse—
    To-morrow's Ladies' Night.
      I learned this wisdom from my mother:
        I teach it to my sons:
      'Choose sometimes one and sometimes t'other,
        But never both at once.'

    The Punch Guide to Good Living; n.d.
      (A *Punch* anthology, circa 1973)

The Boom in Beaumes

Robin and Judith Yapp

S IX kilometres south of Gigondas lies the small town of Beaumes-de-Venise, a jumble of golden-yellow houses and cottages surmounted by the grey ruins of the château, sprawling over the steep slope of the farther side of the Dentelles de Montmirail. The centre of Beaumes is marked by a splendid Provençal fountain and a busy bar-restaurant, the Lou Castelet. Here the accommodation is simple and cheap, the food good, and the atmosphere welcoming. The vineyard workers gather in the bar after their day's toil to converse, to play a curious local dice game, and to take an apéritif before their evening meal. Our theory, that whilst the French make the best wines in the world, it is the English who best know how to consume them, is upheld here in Beaumes. That golden-amber liquid in each glass is the most important product of the town, the gorgeous, tangy, flavoursome Muscat de Beaumes-de-Venise. The men who make it drink the wine as a precursor to a meal and not, as any self-respecting Englishmen would know by instinct, as a dessert wine. The road from Gigondas to Carpentras, the D7, skirts Beaumes to the west. Here, near the church tower of Notre Dame d'Aubune, a co-operative, built in 1956, makes a delightful and consistent example. The director, M. Paulo, enthusiastically explains its vinification, and demonstrates the care with which it is made. The *muscat à petits-grains* is picked in October, when fully ripe. The rich, tawny colour of the muscat results from the inclusion of five per cent of black grapes. Rich in sugar (they must have at least two hundred and fifty-two grammes per litre of juice) they are de-stalked in the *égrappoir*, and pressed. The juice passes through a cooling machine, to enter the concrete tanks at 0°C. Fermentation takes ten or twelve days, during which the temperature rises to between ten and twelve degrees C, and any

solid matter sinks to the bottom. The next stage, the *mutage*, is cru-
cial. At precisely the right moment, when the newly-formed wine
has one hundred and twenty-five grammes of sugar per litre, fermentation must be arrested by the addition of 97° alcohol in exactly the
correct proportion. The end result, a powerful wine with an intense
fragrance that is almost pungent, and a formidable 21° of alcohol,
is sealed into ornately moulded bottles with metal screwtops. These
are sensible, as the contents of a part-used bottle will not deteriorate
for several weeks, especially if kept in a refrigerator.

Here I must explain that for the past nearly twenty years, first
with my late brother, now with my wife, I have been shipping, com-
mercially, the wines of the Rhône and the Loire: it was after our first
shipment of this delicious wine, in 1969, that Elizabeth David sent
us her congratulations, pointing out though, that we were wrong to
suppose that we were the first to import it: Gerald Asher, who had
made a reputation for himself as the first really serious shipper of
wines from the lesser-known parts of France, had introduced it to
British wine-lovers five years before, and she had welcomed it in one
of her weekly *Spectator* articles in January 1964.

Anyway, we found ourselves with a success on our hands, for
there was a commercial consequence to the stability of a dessert
wine so high in natural sugar and in alcohol: its keepability – to coin
a word – once the bottle had been opened meant that it could safely
be offered in restaurants by the glass, and restaurants discovered a
British taste for a drop of something sweet, yet lighter (and cheaper)
than port, to go with pudding. In no time at all, it seemed, Beaumes-
de-Venise had become something of a cult – so much so that one of
the trendy glossy magazines felt called upon to rebuke hostesses for
forgetting the existence of other dessert wines.

＊   ＊   ＊   ＊

Meanwhile, we had been visiting and revisting Beaumes, and discovering that much as we admired (and sold) the co-operative's
luscious wine, the product of a privately-owned vineyard, using
only its own grapes, could show more elegance and finesse than the
blend from many growers. We fell in love with the individually-
made Muscat of the Domaine de Durban – a nuanced, thought-pro-
voking, sipping sort of wine, perhaps to be enjoyed on warm summer nights out of doors, compared with its more assertive, robust

cousin from the co-operative, full enough in character to partner the most unctuous of puddings.

Domaine de Durban is hard to find. After an hour and more spent searching the hills towards Mont Ventoux, we found the track that mounts for three kilometres into the Dentelles de Montmirail. High on a plateau hidden in the hills is the impressive estate of Jacques Leydier. He is one of the few growers who kept alive the making of traditional Muscat between the two World Wars. Until the grant of *appellation* in 1945, M. Leydier and his friends would pick the fully-ripe grapes in mid-October and lay them on straw mats to ripen further before pressing. The more controllable method employed today must make his life relatively easier, and the Leydiers seem to make a splendid wine every year.

In Roman times, the discovery of a sulphur spring led to the establishment of a small spa, called Urban—hence the modern name. As recently as the last century at least seventy people lived here, but now all that remains is the Leydiers' fine house. At such an altitude, water supply is a problem. The ancient cistern, or reservoir, of the former village forms part of the house, and is still of tremendous value during the long, hot Provençal summer. More amazing yet, the *cuverie* below the elegant sitting-room was the subterranean chapel of the small community, as the vaulted roof and tiny gothic window high in one wall testify. The chapel is now devoted to the secular ceremony of the vinification of the Leydiers' transcendental wine. At an altitude of four hundred and forty metres, Jacques's vines are less beset by the maladies to which the *muscat* is notoriously prone than those of his less fortunate colleagues on the plain below. Only white grapes, *grains-blancs*, are used to form the green-gold miracle of Durban. Even the charming and intelligent Leydiers, makers of such nectar (in our opinion, comparable with the best dessert wines of the Sauternais or Loire) will still offer you their superb product as an apéritif. They are prepared, however, to concede the wine's valuable place as the appropriate termination of a fine repast and, further, to urge their clients to conserve the wine. The Leydiers feel that twenty years should not be too long to wait for eventual reflective and reverential enjoyment, though we think they realise that a lot of us can't wait...

Vineyards and Vignerons, 1979

Wine in General

John Hackett

Y love affair with wine began in my teens when we lived in Adelaide. We had for a while a butler who enjoyed looking after me in the holidays when I was often alone at the table.

Largely because of German immigration, several generations back, there is good wine to be had in South Australia. Names like Quellthaler tell their story. My family knew old-established vintners, who told us that they could produce much better wine than they marketed, but that hardly anyone seemed to want it. They made a little for themselves and their friends and shipped most of the rest overseas, sending quantities of rough and ready red stuff to, of all places, Bordeaux.

I remember well a milestone in my progress, now more than fifty years ago. I was on my way up to Oxford and my father took me off the P & O ship at Marseilles and, before catching the Blue Train, gave me a bouillabaisse with a bottle of Meursault Goutte d'Or: one of the four most memorable bottles I can recall, with food I shall never forget. My introduction to that cinnamon-coloured mud with

all the marvellous mysterious fishy things in it, and my share of a
bottle of golden glory, opened a new chapter.

It was at Oxford, however, that the affair took off. There was
(and is) some gorgeous claret under the old buildings and much
other good wine besides, though it was the claret (with some attention to port) that I principally went for.

I read what I could and remember the pleasure of discovering
George Saintsbury (now, I am told, thought rather old-fashioned)
and Maurice Healy; of finding out how 'Clairet', the lighter of the
two red wines made in Gascony, became 'Claret'; and of speculating
whether Haut Brion, standing in flattish country with no Bas Brion
nearby, really did get its name from the Dublin wine merchant who
sold Bordeaux to the Irish gentry in the eighteenth century (my own
forebears included) and happened to be called O'Brien. I could
recite all the true growths of the Médoc (it is curious to reflect how
little one heard of Pomerol and St Emilion in the early thirties—and
how much one missed) and I grieved over the unjust exclusion of
Mouton Rothschild from the first, though this was to bring me to
the second of my four most memorable bottles.

I went in due course with my regiment, the 8th Hussars, to Cairo
and in the mid-thirties I was dining alone in Shepheard's Grill. A
temporary *sommelier* approved my choice of a bottle of Mouton
Rothschild because it was, he said, a wine of 'the first growth'. My
remonstrance over this touched his professional pride. He insisted,
so I bet him a bottle that he was wrong and after a short reference
to the cellar book got one for nothing. Among memorable contacts
with Bordeaux, I would put close to this bottle of Mouton
Rothschild, the bottle of Haut Brion 1961 which my wife and I
drank only a year or so ago in the Grand Véfour, after many fruitless
attempts to get to this famous place. The wine was magnificent,
beautifully presented, but cost me some £40, while the Cairo bottle
was free.

I think it must have been at Oxford that I announced an intention
to make an important part of my life's work (whatever that might
turn out to be) the collection of Rowlandsons and claret. Alas, fifty
years later, I possess only one Rowlandson and, because thirty-five
of these years were spent as a military nomad I have collected no cellar. I run a sort of wine transit camp, where nothing stays more than
a year or two at most, though there is now some quite good claret,
and even better port.

Oxford was not all claret. John Cheetham, who became an ambassador, and I used to meet on Friday nights at that admirable restaurant, now sadly defunct, the George, to discuss a jugged hare and a bottle of Châteauneuf du Pape. With Wilfred Brinton, now retired as a distinguished consultant physician, I used to frequent the United University Club to drink venerable Madeira, some from 1882. With him, too, I explored sherry. We used to eat at the Spanish restaurant in Swallow Street, Martinez, where the sherry came round in wooden kegs on a trolley. We would start off with a glass of one of the better finos—Tio Pepe perhaps—then order luncheon and, as we ate, scorning the purists' advice against sherry as a table wine, drink our way steadily through what was on offer, with food to match. Manzanilla followed the fino, then Amontillado, Amoroso, the wine getting darker and darker as we went along to end up with Old Solera and Carne de Membrillo. That rich sweet sherry and that lush quince-jelly went together as a natural pair, like vintage port and walnuts, or Rhine wine and peaches, or claret and grouse. I had heard it said by some don that every man, whether he knew it or not, was either a Platonist or an Aristotelian. A division almost as important to me, during the time I was spending on these two ancient men, seemed to be between those who preferred Burgundy with a bird, or Bordeaux. I greatly respect Burgundy but would go for a good Bordeaux every time.

For some years, the normal table wine in my house was Soave for white and Valpolicella for red. Now we drink more Lutomer Riesling than anything, though we never call it that. My wife's family is Austrian and used to live in what they call the 'K and K' times (the 'Königliche und Kaiserliche Zeit') of the Austro-Hungarian Empire, in a place now in Yugoslavia, which was then known as Marburg and is now called Maribor. This Riesling, made not far away, was then called Luttenberger and that is what we call it. I order several dozen of Lutomer Riesling every month but what we drink at home is Luttenberger.

We know the wines of Austria well, from those that travel easily (and these do not seem to be many) to others like the pink Schilcher of Steiermark that do not travel at all. Most are best drunk near where they are made, better out of a jug than a bottle—Grüner Velt-liner, for example, shining green-gold with a tiny sparkle, from a generous glass, or Blauburgunder in the Burgenland. Our frequent sojourns in my wife's beautiful native land have left me with a persistent habit. I call it my 'Continental breakfast': every summer now in England, when the peaches come in from abroad, our invariable breakfast of a soft boiled egg, wholemeal toast, fresh ground coffee and home-made marmalade, is preceded, for me, by a peach and a glass of white wine. If it is Austrian wine so much the better. It is usually Luttenberger.

I spoke of four memorable bottles and have mentioned only two. A third came my way a year before World War II, at the bottom of the Jordan Valley, after a midsummer day which my cavalry squadron of the Trans-Jordan Frontier Force had spent riding through a furnace of brown cliffs and burning stone on an anti-bandit operation. At nightfall, the commander came down from the cooler uplands by car, bringing with him my great friend Bob Coates of the Coldstream. Bob had an ice-bucket and in it a bottle of ice-cold champagne. I have never drunk anything more beautiful. Of course, if you have not been conditioned by riding since before dawn in high summer along Jordan's almost treeless bank, 1,000 feet below sea level, where the heat hits you like a hammer, you will not want your wine so cold. I often rescue the bottle from the ice bucket in a restaurant before the wine comes to taste of nothing.

My fourth memorable bottle? In September 1943, the parachute brigade I was commanding was to capture the port of Taranto in Southern Italy from the sea, landing for the assault in very light order. The whole of Brigade HQ's paper was locked up in one office box, which travelled with a couple of staff officers and me in that gallant ship *HMS Penelope*, under her gallant captain, Belben, both later lost off Anzio. I shall always remember watching from *Penelope's* bridge as the Italian battle fleet steamed out of Taranto, under escort from *HMSs Howe* and *King George V*, while we were moving in. Captain Belben gave me as a parting present his last bottle of Tio Pepe. The only place to stow this was the office box, already over-full. Something had to go. The choice was easy. No one could tell me anything important or anything I wanted to hear over the rear-link-radio from a Divisional HQ, already out of range behind us. I turned the codes out of the box and gave them to the Captain in exchange for the fino. Within the hour we were fighting a German parachute rearguard on Taranto's wharves. We drank the fino later.

The most memorable wine drinking occasion of my life was a state banquet at Buckingham Palace. I was an ADC-General to the

Queen. It was a splendid occasion, with over a hundred guests, gold plate for the hot dishes and Sèvres settings for the rest. The service was from men in the royal livery, each with only a few guests to look after.

'Sherry, Sir John?' said a velvety voice over my right shoulder, as the soup came up in its gold plate. 'Thank you: I'd like some sherry'. Then Balmoral salmon and the velvet voice again. 'Hock, Sir John?' 'Thank you: I have been looking forward to this Johannisberger.' 'It will not disappoint you, Sir John.'

Something else to eat. 'Claret, Sir John?' 'Thank you; it is good to meet this Margaux.' 'You will find it a noble wine, Sir John.'

The ice pudding arrived. 'Château Yquem, Sir John, or champagne?' 'I have a difficulty here; I should love the Yquem but what I really think I need is a glass of champagne.'

'Then may I make the suggestion, Sir John, that I give you both?'

Excellent man. I never at any time saw his face but the trust between us was complete.

My last thought is with sherry. A close friend gave me a fino, which I recognised as Garvey's San Patricio— delicious but expensive. 'Averil's cooking wine,' said my friend. 'You don't mean your dear wife cooks with this?' 'Not at all,' was the reply, 'it's only that she will not cook without it.'

Footnote: I was correcting this proof on my birthday. Out of the blue came a tele-message: 'Very many Happy Returns. A case of cooking sherry awaits you. Much love, Tony and Averil...'

ON THE
HOUSE

Front Bench Looks Back

Roy Hattersley

I REMEMBER the tops far more clearly than I recall the tastes. Orange squash had tin that screwed on to the outside of the bottle neck. A Birmingham backstreet workshop had stamped it out of such thin metal that the edges were as sharp as a razor blade and, once removed, it was so easily crushed out of shape that it was usually impossible to replace it. Its cheap destructibility carried with it the compensating advantage of making it necessary to drink all the sticky liquid at once, lest it should – through its topless exposure – lose the few bubbles that had been pumped into it.

Tizer was quite the opposite. Its iron-stone stopper was wholly indestructible and, with the aid of a protuberance that curved out from its top like the crest of a fireman's helmet, could be firmly twisted tight inside of the bottle's neck after every gulp. Lemonade had humble corks that were only partly disguised by a piece of Bakelite bearing the maker's name and address that was attached to their tops. Sometimes they were fastened to the bottles with wire as if they were too precious to lose. The fancy drinks that claimed a vicarious connection with cherries, raspberries and pineapples, had press-on lever-off serrated caps that were no better than what you might find on a bottle of cheap ale. But ah, ginger beer ...!

Ginger beer was different.

At least, some ginger beer was. At Hemmings (groceries) English's (fruit and vegetables) and the 'beer-off' ('off licence' as it would have been known in the outside world) there was nothing special about any of the soft drink bottles except the soda-syphons. And we only allowed ourselves to think about them when grandma was mortally ill, and then we worried about the one-and-sixpence deposit. But at Glen Howe – a park with a trout stream that was

152

owned, a mysterious two miles away, by the West Riding County Council – they had on sale full pints of ginger beer in containers of almost unimaginable mechanical ingenuity.

The neck of the pale green thick glass bottles contained a ball of darker green glass, the size of an emperor marble. At the moment of purchase the jade sphere was pressed tight in the top of the bottle neck. Indeed for years, I believed that it had been blown up there by the effervescence of the ginger beer – a view reinforced by the bubbles in the glass ball that I attributed not to its inferior quality but to the pressures from below in the bottle forcing particles of gas into its solid mass.

Such bottles were opened with a specially constructed wooden contraption which was placed over the neck of the bottle and struck with the palm of the hand, thus pushing the glass ball down into a wider chamber within the neck and allowing the ginger beer to gurgle out around it. In theory – indeed, in practice – the marble could be knocked back with a suitable shaped object, a clothes peg, the pointed end of a cricket stump or even the thing for getting stones out of horses' hooves that was attached to every decent penknife. But the purveyors of such bottles always, in my experience, insisted on opening them with the patent device.

Perhaps they were worried about the likes of me smashing their precious bottles in our attempts to force them open with scout poles or walking sticks. They may have even been concerned in case, having affected forcible entry at the bottles' expense, we had decided that the ginger beer was too precious to waste and risked death either from oral bleeding or poison by powdered glass. Whatever their motive – and it may have just been commercial – once the glass ball was pushed down into the bottle the whole contents had to be swigged down, polished off or whatever was the *patois* of the day for drunk.

Indeed, one of the reasons why the memories of the bottles have outlasted the memories of their contents was that the bottles lasted for so much longer. There must have been half-full bottles of Tizer ('the appetiser') and lemonade in my young life, but I can only remember the empties – twopence on every one that we returned, but sometimes kept to carry water on our more frugal walks and poverty-stricken picnics. Nor can I remember the glasses from which we drank at home. I know that we used thin tumblers, for I can remember longing to suck through straws – a habit that my mother thought both an affectation and an extravagance, since the glasses were already in our possession and straws had to be bought.

During adolescence, I graduated from bottles bought in grocers' shops and consumed at home, to glasses consumed on the premises of what were called pop-shops. They called themselves herbalists and existed to sell liquorice root, senna pods and various other dubious remedies. As a side-line they dispensed glasses of sarsparilla to young men who were on their way to the fish-and-chip shop or from the municipal tennis courts. One of my tennis-playing, chip-eating, drinking companions no doubt recognised horizontal diversification when he saw it, for he has become Sir Peter Middleton KCB, Permanent Secretary to the Treasury.

My mother worried that the occasional call at the pop-shop would leave me perilously poised at the top of the well-oiled slope that led directly down to a nightly visit to the local public house. In fact, it had generally beneficial effects. For it acted as a sort of aversion therapy, alienating me forever from thick, sweet, brown drinks. In the 1940s nothing called cola – either Pepsi or Coca – ever passed our lips. But whenever I see it now, I shy away in memory of the bags of aniseed and packets of laburnum leaves in the 'pop shop'. The colas also come in self-opening tins and squashy plastic bottles. There can be no romance about a soft drink served in such inelegant containers. Even if I expected to like their taste, to drink them would be a betrayal of Tizer screw tops and the ginger-beer glass balls of my heavy drinking days.

Liberal Sees Red

Clement Freud

MY local street market is currently overwhelmed with beefsteak tomatoes. They are called by that name not because they taste of meat – indeed, they taste of very little – but because they are large and, when served with a steak, take up great parts of the plate which would otherwise (I mean if a smaller tomato was deployed) have to be filled with more expensive steak.

Tomatoes were once a rare and respected fruit, of the South American nightshade family. To say they caught on is an understatement. They are now with us 365 days a year and in leap years will be with us on February 29th also. Familiarity breeds contempt (familiarity also breeds, though this is irrelevant to the argument) and the ubiquity of the tomato, served grilled for breakfast, in soup form at lunch, sliced in sandwiches at tea-time and dressed as a salad as a favoured supper dish, has actually diminished its popularity. Nobody much cares for tomatoes; they just eat them, mainly because they are there, because horticulturalists and Italians grow them against the consumer. Tons and latterly tonnes of them, ever redder, ever blander, as if there were some sort of distinction in being able to produce something from the ground that tastes as if it has been manufactured, flood the markets of the western world.

Tomato soup, that chemical breakthrough whereby caramel and seasoning, colouring and monosodium glutamate make people stretch their eyes and say, 'Now that's what I call a tomato taste,' shows that you can fool all the people all the time. Tinned tomatoes, queuing by the container-load to get out of Italy and into intervention stock, contain tomato, salt and water. It is a moot point whether it is worth sending them north, for the farmers get the same EEC largesse if they plough them back into the land. And yet, every now and again, you come across a real tomato which tastes of sun-shine and good husbandry, and you forgive their kinsfruit for their perennial dreariness.

The Mediterranean tomato is probably the most reliable, but caring greengrocers, who have been known to taste produce before selling it to the public, are found from time to time and must be encouraged by enthusiastic custom. Should you find such an establishment, there is a natural tendency to manifest the macho image, take the luscious tomato in the right hand and slam the whole shebang into your mouth. On careful consideration, you will discover that the quality lies in the pulp, and what God was thinking about when he provided skin and pips for nightshade fruit is anyone's guess; gastronomy had no part in the design.

I spent many years reading cook-books that advised folk to remove skin and seeds – and ignoring the advice. I was wrong. I am now converted. You make an incision around the circumference, dip the tomatoes in boiling salted water, lift them out with a slotted spoon 30 seconds later, and the skin wrinkles itself away from the flesh. Taste the skin to see whether it has merit and I am wrong.

Then taste the tomato to see if it is worth continuing; if it is as dull as are the majority, cut the skinned tomatoes into slices, dust them with a little sugar, sprinkle upon each slice a few drops of olive oil, leave in a cool place, and serve with coarse salt and chopped basil. But if it has quality, remove the seeds (taste the seeds to see whether they have merit and I am wrong). You remove the seeds by cutting the fruit into quarters and easing the pips from the flesh with your fingertips, under a slow-running tap of cold water.

You now have the very best part of the very best fruit. It is a sensational base for a tomato sorbet, even better if spiked with a little mint. Mixed with gelatin, it can become a tomato mousse of irresistible allure, and if you are clever and wipe the mould with a thin film of oil, garnish the base with cunningly arranged sprigs of herb, set it, cool it, and decant it on to fine white china, you will have a dish that calls for a colour photographer as well as a Michelin rosette. A sauce made by incorporating Greek yoghourt with mayonnaise and chopped chive would go well with this.

But my favourite tomato-based sauce is produced by cutting high-class pulp into smallish pieces, simmering them for three minutes in virgin olive oil in a pan rubbed with a clove of garlic, and adding no more than a little salt, a few turns of the white peppermill, and basil leaves if they are fresh and perfumed.

It is a sauce that translates boiled potatoes, steamed rice or humble cooked pasta into a dish of the highest quality, and will persuade you to reduce your holdings of tomato purée. Such a sauce can be stored, if there is any left after its first appearance at table, for three to four days in a closed jar in the refrigerator. If it is adventure you seek, spoon some over a poached egg, add a dollop of thick soured cream, and if your guests are hungry rather than interested in gastronomy, serve the egg on a bed of chopped spinach or sorrel.

Tomates Provençales is a dish of small subtlety but huge appeal and needs ingredients of no more than average quality. Six tomatoes; half a stale white loaf; 3ozs of butter and much salt and parsley.

Generously butter the oven dish and place the halved tomatoes therein, well seasoned, flat sides up. Liquidise the bread into crumbs. Add parsley and salt, mix in the butter, melted, and strew generously over the tomatoes. Bake until the top is crisp – when the bottom will be cooked.

Many calories, hardly any cost, no skill. I can think of few better winter ways of supporting the tomato-grower.

Punch, 18 September 1985

The Tipplings of a Travelling Tory

Julian Critchley

L IKE some legendary north-country Alderman, when it comes to wine, I know what I like. Twenty years of silent service on the back benches and the hazards of public life have also taught me what to avoid. The great ones, who travel the world in black Rovers nursing red boxes entitle their slim volumes of memoirs *The View from the Bridge* or *The Hand on the Tiller*; the not so great, victims of a thousand Rotary-club lunches, will call their autobiographies *Spanish Sauternes* – a tribute by the unspeakable to the undrinkable.

No politician is at his best on his feet. He comes into his own at the constituency luncheon or 'supper', where, seated next to the wife of the Mayor of Casterbridge, he discusses life on the Costa del Sol while toying with tomato soup from a packet, the undissolved grounds of which cling to the side of the bowl with the tenacity of first wives. The rolls are hard, but not so hard as the lamb, which has been cooked some hours before and then reheated. The potatoes are tinned and the broccoli frozen. Circumstances such as these make the public man, faced with having to reply to the toast of the Guests, greet twin bottles of 'red' and 'white' plonked down before him with the enthusiasm of a lover reunited. What does it matter that the 'burgundy' is from Albania or that the Muscadet is as purse-lipped and flinty as Mrs Thatcher rebuking Harold Stockton. Enoch Powell claimed that humbug is the lubricant of public life. He was wrong.

Although some Tories are wet in the constituencies, we are rarely dry in the Palace of Varieties in Westminster. In the dear, dead days, when elderly Knights of the Shire with names like Sir Hugh Munro-Lucas-Tooth and Sir Jocelyn Lucas served on the Wine Committee, a select body that assumed the burden of choosing the Commons' wine, travelled in the heat of the day to Burgundy and Bordeaux, giving freely of their services. In 1965, Robert Maxwell, then an obstreperous back-bench Labour MP, was made chairman of the Kitchen Committee, with a brief to balance the books. Maxwell sold off the contents of the cellar and brought in a thin list from Grant's of St James – a choice of not much more than a dozen bottles, and precious few halves, the most expensive at about six pounds, not counting champagne, which confronts us to this day. I can tell 'Captain Bob' that his name is more frequently on our lips than his wine...

Only we Tories suffer from drinking cheap wine, whose Gallic acidity makes its own contribution to 'the resolute approach'. Labour constituency parties wisely prefer bottled beer to Yugoslav riesling. Social Democrats on the other hand, as a gesture to 'Mr David', drink either the best of Sainsbury's or a California Chenin Blanc in memory of Paul Masson, whose service to the upwardly mobile classes on both sides of the Atlantic has made his position among Social Democrats analogue to that once held by Disraeli among Conservatives. The Liberals, however, drink home-made wine out of their sandals as a gesture to community politics.

I must take care not to paint too grim a picture. Conservative students may drink Tartan Ale out of cans while putting the torch to some Edinburgh polytechnic, but the more mature members of our great party can, despite the perils of campaigning for re-election, tell a Chénas from a Rully. This could be accounted for by ancestral memory, but is more likely due to two factors: the hospitality of lobbyists of all kinds; and the opportunity of service in Europe, at the European 'Parliament', the Council of Europe and the Western European Union. Service abroad has two advantages denied to those who stay at home to look after the talking shop; the food is better and the oratory incomprehensible.

Were you to glance into New Palace Yard around lunch time on any weekday, you would see a queue of MPs waiting impatiently for cabs. Voices, proletarian or proud, command conveyance to the Savoy or the Connaught where, while toying with a sole Dieppoise, MPs will listen with but half an ear to the supplications of their hosts, who generally have something to sell. It is on occasions like these that we are permitted to drink above our station, the tentative suggestion of a Chablis being countered by a query as to the name of the shipper, a piece of one-upmanship which can convert, as if by magic, an undistinguished bottle into a Chablis Grand Cru Vaudésir '76. We were not born yesterday.

In 1972, I was asked by the whips whether I would like to go to Europe. I accepted and spent seven years of exile abroad in receipt of a regular income paid by the Party trustees.

I flew by chartered aircraft to Paris and Strasbourg. In Alsace, I would sit silently on the terraces of cafes, sipping Gewurztraminer and gazing fixedly at the distant blue line of the Vosges. In my modest hotel, the Gutenberg, I kept a bottle of Riesling Special Reserve in the bidet. At night I would toss fitfully, roused at intervals by the cathedral bells, troubled by onion tart, *matelote à la crème* and knuckle of pork, the whole churning rebuke having been watered with the mouth-puckering *vins de pays*. On Sundays the jaded Parliamentarians would board buses for *un tour des vins d'Alsace* returning late at night to their narrow beds. I am still fond of Strasbourg and there are many worse aperitifs than a well-chilled Gewurz.

In Paris I went up in the world. I was lucky enough to run into my old bank manager who had, in the early 'fifties, doled out my 30,000 francs a month, a parental subvention that kept me more or less in the vicinity of the Sorbonne. Twenty years later he invited me to stay with him on my twice-yearly visits, an invitation which would have been generous enough had he been a teetotaller. In fact, he sat on a cellar which was one of the best in France, a collection that had begun with the purchase of the bankrupt stock of a great restaurant in Bordeaux. The Laws-Johnsons gave a dinner party for me twice a year. Vera would do the cooking; something relatively simple like charcuterie, chicken and rice and a superb plate of cheeses, a sensible backdrop to the wines. I made a note in my diary of the wines served, and I give examples not to boast but to marvel: on one occasion after the champagne, we drank Meursault '44, a magnum of La Mission Haut Brion '50, Mouton Rothschild '34 and a golden Château Climens '47; on another a magnum of Cheval Blanc '47, described as the finest bottle of claret ever. The guests were French and British; we marvelled, but the natives were astounded, for it appears that only the great wine families of France drink really well.

The Parliamentary delegation abroad, favourite of married MPs, must depend very largely on *les vins de pays*. In 1964 I went to Ethiopia. We dined with the Emperor on *quat* and light ale – Bass – but, having travelled the Empire, we spent the last two days recuperating at the Imperial Guest House. A knight of the shire, who had a nose for that sort of thing, discovered a cache of noble claret. We sat peacefully in the garden watching the sun set into the Sudan, sipping Lafite and eating goat's cheese and unleavened bread. Those who would taste *la douceur de la vie* should have known Ethiopia before the Revolution.

At home, the better sort of Conservative MP is sometimes invited to lunch by the Government Hospitality Department. The reward for listening to a speech by some visiting dignitary and the response by Sir Geoffrey, is a decent burgundy of the sort drunk today only by Japs and degenerate sheiks. The choice of the Government's wine lies in the hands of Lord Gladwyn, one Liberal who has never made his own.

I am consoled by my memories. Life has not always been a bottle of Blue Nun, or half a carafe of House of Commons red wine, drunk in the company of a junior minister whose conversation swings between a description of his constituency ward boundaries, and the assertion that he, at least, can see a light at the end of the tunnel. And there is no lobbyist, however vile, one's pleasure in whose company cannot be improved by a decent bottle. Even the prospect of eventually having to fight a general election – all that wine and all that cheese – can be softened by the prospect of a Corton Charlemagne drunk in the open air in the company of a pretty woman. O lachryma, o Christi...

SOME MEMORABLE MEALS

It Isn't Only Peaches Down in Georgia

Harry Luke

I T was my fortune in 1920, when I was British Chief Commissioner in the three Trans-Caucasian Republics of Georgia, Armenia and Azerbaijan, to be entertained at many typical Caucasian banquets, a process that required on the part of the stranger some training and a certain corporal elasticity if it was to be undergone without disaster. How the Georgian officers of those days retained their greyhound figures despite the quantities they ate and drank was a mystery I could explain to myself only by means of the vigorous *pas seuls* they would execute between courses.

These banquets, which never got under way until at least two hours after the time for which one had been bidden, began with cold *zakuski* (hors d'oeuvres), eaten standing and washed down with small glasses of vodka. The *zakuski* were always so appetizing that the uninitiated were apt to leave insufficient accommodation for what was to follow. Fresh caviare straight from Baku, bears' hams, mushrooms steeped in wine, smoked river-trout, salmon and tongues and every other conceivable savoury dish, were an irresistible temptation to the unwary, largely thanks to the fact that good vodka (for there are many grades, ranging from wheat vodka to that made of wood pulp) is the world's perfect apéritif. That is to say that it creates and stimulates an appetite which, even if artificially induced, at least never flags while the process continues and is never known—at all events in my experience—to result in the least suggestion of a hangover provided that only the best vodka is used.

One then passed into another room to sit down to the hot *zakuski*, which were an ample meal in themselves. They consisted first of pheasant or partridge soup in which one soaked large game pasties handed round separately; next of the delicious variety of salmon-trout found only in lovely Lake Gyökché on the borders of Georgia and Armenia and aptly known as *ishkhan*, the Armenian word for 'prince'; then (the menu in the hot *zakuski* rooms of Tiflis was nearly always the same) of kidneys stewed in sour cream and a Madeira-type wine from the Crimea. And it was only after this more than adequate preparation, as the Western European might suppose, that one entered the dining-room and sat down to the real meal of the evening.

At this stage it was the amiable custom of one's Georgian hosts to drink—to the accompaniment of cries of *Allah verdi*, the Turkish and Tatar for 'God has given'—the health of the visitors in a pony-glass of wine, which had to be lowered without heel-taps by both toaster and toastee and demanded quite definite powers of endurance on the part of the visitors if the hosts, as in the case of a military mess, were many. For each host claimed, and exercised, his privilege. My friend Prince Napoleon Murat, great-grandson of Joachim Murat, Napoleon's Marshal and subsequently King of Naples, and grandson on his mother's side of the last Queen of Mingrelia, told me in Tiflis—he was then a General in the Georgian Army—that when he left the French Army to go to Russia as an officer of the Imperial *gardes à cheval*, his new Russian brother-officers welcomed him at a banquet which lasted uninterruptedly for two nights and the intervening day.

The Tenth Muse, 1950

Victorian Dinner-Party

E.F. Benson

CERTAINLY I could never have witnessed a dinner-party in the early seventies, but I seem to know a great deal about it, partly from having been permitted by the butler to observe the magnificent preparations for it, partly from having personally watched through the banisters of the gallery that overhung the hall the arrival of the guests, and partly from having been told later by my mother the manner of these gargantuan feasts. But I can testify how immense was the perspective of the monstrous, round-backed mahogany chairs of the period that lined the elongated dining-room table. Upon it stood a pair of branched candelsticks and other lesser lights, and for centre-piece there was a wondrous silver epergne. Upon the ornamental base of it reclined a camel with a turbaned Arab driver: he leaned against the trunk of a tall palm-tree that soared upwards straight and bare for a full eighteen inches. At the top of this majestic stem there spread out all round the feathery fronds of its foliage, and resting on them (though in reality firmly screwed into the top of the palm-trunk) stood a bowl of cut glass filled with moist sand. In this was planted a bower of honeysuckle which trailed over the silver leaves of the palm-tree and completed the oasis for the Arab and his camel.

Along the long dining-room wall stood a great oak sideboard below a steel engraving of the 'Last Supper' by Leonardo da Vinci: beside this hung another steel engraving of the Prince Consort with his wide-awake in his hand. This sideboard had two fine panels from some sixteenth-century reredos let into the back, and the artificers of Wardour Street had built up the rest round them: it was considered very handsome. On it stood a row of decanters of port, sherry, and claret, and the dessert service made by Copeland, late Spode. And now the tapestry curtains were drawn with a clash of rings over the windows, and the candles were lit, and I was haled away from this glittering cave of Aladdin and hurried upstairs on the first sound of the front-door bell, breathlessly to watch from the passage that ran round the hall, the arrival of the splendid guests. The men put down their hats and coats in the outer hall and then waited by the fireplace of the inner hall (of which through the banisters, not over them, I commanded so admirable a view) for the emergence of their ladies from my mother's sitting-room where the work-boxes and lazy-tongs had been put away and pins and brushes and looking-glasses provided for their titivation. They had gone in mere chrysalides, swathed in shawls and plaids; they emerged magnificent butterflies, all green and pink and purple. As each came floating forth, her husband offered her his arm and they went thus into the drawing-room. When all were assembled the gong boomed, and out they came again, having changed partners, and the galaxy passed into the glittering cave of Aladdin next door. Grace was said, and they sat down to the incredible banquet.

There was thick soup and clear soup (a nimble gourmand had been known to secure both). Clear soup in those days had a good

deal of sherry in it. There was a great boiled turbot with his head lolling over one end of the dish, and his tail over the other: then came a short pause, while at the four corners of the table were placed the four *entrées*. Two were brown *entrées*, made of beef, mutton, or venison, two were white *entrées* made of chicken, brains, rabbit, or sweetbreads, and these were handed round in pairs ('Brown or White, Madam?'). Then came a joint made of the brown meat which had not figured in the brown *entrées*, or if only beef and mutton were in season, the joint might be a boiled ham. My mother always carved this herself instead of my father: this was rather daring, rather modern, but she carved with swift artistic skill and he did not, and she invariably refused the offer of her neighbouring gentlemen to relieve her of her task. Then came a dish of birds, duck or game, and a choice followed between substantial puddings and more airy confections covered with blobs of cream and jewels of angelica and ornamental sugarings. A Stilton cheese succeeded and then dessert. My mother collected the ladies' eyes, and the ladies collected their fans and scent-bottles and scarves, and left the gentlemen to their wine. Smoking was not dreamed of at the after-dinner services of this date: the smell would assuredly hang about the dining-room, and no gentleman could possibly talk to a lady in the drawing-room after he had thus befouled himself. When he wished to smoke later on in the evening, he always changed his dinner-coat lest it should get infected ever so faintly with the odour so justly abhorred by the other sex, and put on a smoking-jacket, very smart, padded and braided and befrogged, while for fear that his hair should be similarly tainted, he wore a sort of embroidered forage-cap. Thus attired for his secret and masculine orgy, he slipped from his bedroom after the ladies had gone upstairs and with his flat candle in hand joined his fellow conspirators, as in a charade, in some remote pantry or gun-room, where his padded coat would keep him fairly warm.

In these festive evenings of the seventies prolonged drinking of port and claret had gone out, smoking had not yet come in, and so when the decanters of port and claret had gone round twice, and sherry had been offered (it was called a white-wash), the host rang the bell for coffee. The men then joined the ladies, and the ladies who had been chattering together in a bunch, swiftly broke up, like scattered globules of quicksilver, so that next each of them should be a vacant chair, into which a man inserted himself, avoiding those who had been his neighbours at dinner. A number of conversational duets then took place, but these did not last long, for there was certain to be a lady present who sang very sweetly, or had a lovely 'touch' on the piano (indeed it was more probable that they all sang and played delightfully), and now it was her hour, and her hostess entreated her to play one of those beautiful 'Songs without Words' by Mr. Mendelssohn, who had taught music to Queen Victoria, or sing a song with words. She was not sure if she had brought her music, but it always turned out that her husband had done so and had left the portfolio with his hat and coat in the outer hall. By the time he returned with the melodious volume, another gentleman had escorted her to the piano and had been granted the privilege of turning over for her. She explained that she was terribly out of practice as she put down on the candle-brackets of the piano her gloves, and her fan, her handkerchief and, if she was about to play, her rings and her bracelets also, and thus stripped for the fray she cleared her throat, and ran her fingers up and down the keys with the much-admired 'butterfly touch,' as a signal for the clatter of talk to cease. The audience assumed expressions of regretful melancholy if the music was sad, or of pensive gaiety if it was lively, and fixed their eyes on various points of the ceiling: the more musical instinctively beat time with their fingers or their fans. A brilliant execution was not considered very important, for music was an 'elegant' accomplishment: touch and expression were more highly esteemed, a little tremolo in the voice was most affecting, and these were also easier to acquire than execution. Sentimentality was, in these concerts, the quality most appreciated, and if a lady could induce the female portion of her audience surreptitiously to wipe a slight moisture from its eyes, and the males to clear their throats before, at the end of the performance, there rose the murmur of 'Oh, thank you, what a treat. Please don't get up yet!' she was stamped as an artist, the music as a masterpiece, and the audience as persons of sensibility. Such songs as 'The Lost Chord' (words by my cousin Adelaide Anne Procter, music by Arthur Sullivan) were accepted as test-pieces for tears: the singer tried her strength with them, as if they were punching-machines at a fair which registered muscular force. If there was not a dry eye in the room when she had delivered her blow she was a champion. Men, on these occasions, were not asked to sing, unless they were notable comics: serious playing and singing were purely feminine accomplishments.

Or if (rarely) there was no music, there might be a game of some sort. Whist was unsociable and demanded close attention; besides, in those days young women, it was well known, did not as a rule possess the sort of brain that could grapple with its problems, and were liable to trump their partner's best cards, or not trump their worst. 'Floral Lotto' was far easier, both sexes could play that, and it was very exciting to see your card covered with pictures of the common flowers of the garden gradually filling up. But whatever the diversions, they were all brief, for at 10 o'clock in came a hissing urn and the tea-table was spread. The gentlemen handed the ladies cups of tea, and little hot cakes and buns ('Might I recommend you one of these with sugar on the top?'), and they nibbled and sipped and indulged in lively conversation, in order to restore themselves after the harrowing emotions caused by 'The Lost Chord' ('Beautifully sung, was it not? Such expression!') After tea, perhaps another lady sang, or she who had made them cry or clear their throats with 'The Lost Chord' was prevailed on just as the first carriage was announced, to give them 'The Summer Shower,' and this she did in so arch and playful a manner that everybody felt young and happy again instead of luxuriously miserable, and hummed the tune as they put on their wraps and rumbled away with smiles and compliments and firm incredulity at the lateness of the hour.

As We Were, 1930

Corporate Luncheon

Roy Fuller

The tail-coated banqueting *maître d'hôtel*
Proffers a napkin round potato crisps.

I wave the thing away, but later think
That they were very likely rather good,

Far above even the packets sold by Marks,
The venue being a room at the Savoy.

Not many chances now remain to try
The delicacies of the Baghdad of the West,

Being, as I am, merely a year or two
From total superannuation. I

Seem to myself more than a bit *blasé*.
Though if this is giving up the world, declining

To sully scotch and soda with sliced, fried spuds,
No monstrous hardships wait for me hereafter.

The Spectator, 24 August 1985

Returning to the Sauce

Bernard Levin

WHEN an anthology of my columns was published some time ago, one of the reviewers (he was one of the more sympathetic among them, too) gave thanks that I had not included any of what he called my 'food pornography', no article on 'some disgusting, French-sauce-smothered meal'. This, as Bertie Wooster used to say, made the old head swim a bit; there really are thoughtful and understanding people, lovers of the arts and perceptive analysts of the human condition, who believe that to enjoy good food, and to say so, is literally obscene. Note that in the case of this particular commentator—Mr Christopher Booker—we are not dealing with an instance of all-embracing philistinism, of the genuine hatred of art in all its manifestations displayed by, say, *Private Eye*; many's the refreshing and stimulating conversation about music and books I have had with Mr Booker. Yet when it comes to the art of gastronomy—not to be compared with literature or painting, of course, but an art without doubt, and one which in its practitioners calls for, and receives, the dedication and creativeness of any other artist—what I hear when I discuss it is on one hand the squealing of stuck prigs, which I do not mind about, and on the other the fastidious disdain of Mr Booker, which I do.

Of course, those are not the only tones I hear. Among the letters I get when I write a column on food there are always some from correspondents who either wish to exchange their own views and reminiscences of the subject or who—and this I find more interesting and significant—declare that they cannot themselves afford such experiences but are always pleased to read about mine: in this attitude they are identical, even down to the phraseology, to those correspondents who write to say that they cannot get to Covent Garden or Salzburg, but take much vicarious pleasure in the stimulation of their own music-loving when I write about some absorbing operatic evening I have spent.

As I say, I do not care about the reaction of the prigs; indeed, I derive a certain satisfaction from the knowledge that I am upsetting them. But I am quite unable to understand the reaction of a cultivated man whose horror at the thought of someone enjoying the pleasures of the palate can lead him to bestialize the experience into 'some disgusting, French-sauce-smothered meal'.

All of which is by way of a warning, akin to the one on the side of the cigarette-packets, about today's column: for those who dislike this sort of thing, this is the sort of thing they dislike. Having recently had business which took me to Freiburg-im-Breisgau, just across the Rhine, I decided to retreat via Illhaeusern, where I dined once more at the Auberge de l'Ill of the brothers Haeberlin, and Belfort, where I lunched for the first time at the Hostellerie du Château Servin, where the hand that rocks the saucepan is that of M Dominique Mathy, who looks, incidentally, about nine years old.

I have written before, and shall no doubt write again, about Paul Haeberlin's salmon *soufflé*. This time, however, I decided to miss it, and chose to start instead with the *ballotine* of sole and eel, accompanied by a Hugel Riesling from the amazing repertoire of Alsace wines the Auberge sports. (There was a bonus: as the *sommelier* presented the bottle for my inspection, a tall, dark man, looking somewhat like Mr Robert Maxwell, passed by. The wine-waiter inclined his head and confided that '*C'est Monsieur Hugel même*'. The least I could do, when I had tasted the precious ichor, was to convey my compliments to its onlie begetter.

The combination of the blander sole with the sharper eel was perfectly judged, as was the sauce (a French sauce, I regret to have to tell Mr Booker, but served at the side, not smothering the fish, if that makes things any better, which I dare say it doesn't), a lovely creamy one sprinkled with caviare.

After that, I went on to the *volaille sautée aux morilles*, which was neither more nor less than what it says, except that the bird was as tender as a bruise, and the little crinkly mushrooms could hardly have been picked earlier than that morning, if not afternoon. I dwelt long upon the wine-list, but in the end felt that the Riesling had been so perfectly matched to the fish, and the memory of its crispness was so enduring, that I could safely repeat it for the chicken; nor did I regret my decision.

Then came revelation; at least it came after the cheese—three local ones, chosen blind but justifying my intrepidity (there was no local goat's cheese, no doubt because there are no local goats, but the ways of the fauna of Europe are a mystery to me). I do not recall having previously seen the *fraises de bois Lutétia* on the menu here before, and it may indeed be a new creation, though I was so overcome by it that when the solicitous M Marc swanned up, clearly thinking I was going to faint from joy, I forgot to ask him. Simmering and bubbling gently in a lovely fruity liquid, the strawberries (also manifestly fresh-picked) hid a surprise; half an inch below the heat, there was a bed of ice-cream, and when I struck it I felt like one who has drilled for oil and found it in quantities beyond the dreams of Rockefeller. The wine lasted; is there *anything* you can't drink Alsace wine with?

I thought it best to have only a light breakfast before setting off for Belfort next day. The town has a striking historical episode to remember, previously quite unknown to me: it was besieged during the Franco-Prussian War and held out for nearly four months, while, as the inscription on the monument says, more than 100,000 shells fell upon it. But the monument is the point; built to commemorate the heroic defence of the town, it is a gigantic lion, made out of huge sandstone blocks, set into the hillside crowned by the citadel from which the resistance was directed. The lion, a most imposing beast (his very nose is about 6ft long) was designed by Frédéric Bartholdi, who was also responsible for the Statue of Liberty, and who was born in Colmar, where I spent the night between dinner and lunch, not failing to visit the Musée d'Unterlinden to see the Mathias Grunewald altarpiece. (There you are, you see; not only does gastrophily lead to the acquisition of knowledge; its sinfulness is mitigated by the opportunities it provides of admiring the products of more respectable art-forms.)

But then I went to lunch. The Hostellerie is a charmingly-appointed hotel, with a gracious dining-room, and exceptionally attentive waiters. I knew something interesting was about to happen to me when I saw that the nibbles accompanying my apéritif included a couple of quail's eggs—just that minute done, too. Nor was my confidence misplaced, for there followed one of the most remarkable meals I have had for a very long time.

I began with *saumon en papillote*, steamed in its parcel with tiny shrimps and a razor-cut *julienne* of vegetables that Michel Guérard himself would have been proud of. The gush of scented steam that emerged when the pillow was stabbed gave a promise that was not belied by the delicacy of the fish and its accompaniments. Unasked, they followed it with a tiny lemon sorbet, dripping with *marc de Bourgogne*, which stunned the palate for a perfectly-judged five minutes, leaving it at the end of that time cleared and tingling for the next dish which was *escalope de foie de canard au vinaigre de framboises*. Having drunk yet more Riesling with the fish, I decided on my first red wine of the trip (obviously I had drunk white in the Ratskeller at Freiburg), but when I began to discuss the clarets, the manageress, with infinite charm and tact, steered me away. What she steered me to was a wine of which I had never so much as heard the name: Kaefferkopf. (There is a mountain in Alsace of that name, and doubtless the grapes grow upon its slopes.) But the duck-liver and the raspberries were exquisitely set off by its powerful body and hint of sweetness.

It was by no means over, for a peal of trumpets (perhaps I imagined the trumpets, though I don't *think* so) preceded a cornucopia of desserts second only to that of Alain Chapel at Mionnay. Unfortunately by then (which was after the cheese, of course) I could manage only two: a gateau of raspberries and citron, the taste flowing on perfectly from the liver, and some more *fraises de bois*, this time in champagne syrup. The Kaefferkopf carried on splendidly.

I made straight for Basle, whence I was flying home. You can eat very well in Basle, but I didn't have time: to tell the shameful truth—how you will laugh at me!—I no longer had the appetite, either. Still, having had two such meals, I thought the least I could do was to tell you about them. I hope I have upset the prigs; I hope I have not upset Christopher. No doubt both, in their respective ways, will let me know.

The Times, 15 May 1980

A McGonagall-type Triolet on the Full Revoltingness of Commercial Fast Food

Gavin Ewart

A great double-deck of pure beef with melting cheese,
                    pickle, ketchup and mustard!
Complete your meal with our crisp French Fries and a
                    cool thick Shake!
Enjoy too the fried jumbo-size jumbo-tough
            breadcrumbed macho legs of the Bustard,
a great double-deck of pure beef with melting cheese,
                    pickle, ketchup and mustard,
with a few lightly boiled rats' foetuses on the side, all
                    masked in creamy custard!
Wash it down with a warm Guinness, topped up with
engine oil – and dunk in it our supermale Elephant Cake,
a great double-deck of pure beef with melting cheese,
                    pickle, ketchup and mustard!
Complete your meal with our crisp French Fries and a
                    cool thick Shake!

The Young Pobble's Guide to his Toes, 1984

NOTE: *The first two lines of this poem are genuine food advertising*
of March 1984 in a London take-away eat-in restaurant.

Good Health!

Cyril Ray

O FF and on during the war, and for a few years afterwards, I rented rooms from an old cock known to gossip-writers – but not to anyone else I ever heard of – as the Squire of Piccadilly. He had been born in the year of the Mutiny, attended Disraeli's funeral, and been too old to be commissioned – as he used to say he had wished – in the fifty thousand horse and foot going to Table Bay in 1899.

He was 93 when, in 1950, his manservant (oh yes, he had a manservant, nearly as old as himself) came to my door, bearing with due reverence a bottle of the Cockburn 1908 – my own birthdate, and a great year not only for people but for port. 'Mr Stone knows you like a glass of wine, sir, and he's been told by his doctor to give up port, so he's giving his cellar away.'

I have wondered for 35 years whether, had he said pooh to the doctor and 'another glass' to his man, Willie Stone would not have lived, as he did, to the age of 101 and three-quarters, or whether another little drink wouldn't have done him any harm for those remaining nine years. And, if it didn't, whether those nine years might have been happier ones.

I shall never know.

Nor have I ever decided whether it is better to be fit and fractious off the bottle or happy and unhealthy on – a lack of decision that results only (according to my loved ones) in my being both fuddled *and* fractious.

Having had a rabbi ancestor, a more recent but still remote early upbringing at the hands of Lancashire Wesleyans, and being as it were rurally diaconal by marriage, my first instincts were to seek oracular advice by the *sortes biblicae*, and a fat lot of use the Good Book is to one of troubled mind. Wine is a mocker, strong drink is raging, saith Solomon – but is this a blanket admonition or is he drawing a distinction between the mere giggles induced by burgundy, say, or champagne, and the horrors brought on by the hard stuff? A little wine, Paul told Timothy, for his stomach's sake, but never mind Tim's tum, what about my liver?

Turning from revealed religion to the miraculous discoveries of modern science, I find in the pages of *Wine, Health and Society, the Proceedings of a Symposium Sponsored by the University of California, the Society of the Medical Friends of Wine and the Wine Institute of San Francisco*, held in November 1981, that so far as my liver is concerned much depends on the kinetics of ethanol absorption, which in turn is conditioned by the reoxidation of NADH,

which occurs chiefly in the microchrondia and the flavoprotein cytochrome system. The acetate is translocated from the liver and is oxidized extrahepatically. The reactions for the NAD system may, as perhaps will already have occurred to you, be summarized by the following:

$$C_2H_5 + NAD \xrightarrow{ADH} CH_3 CHO + NADH$$

$$CH_3 CHO + NADH \xrightarrow{AldDH} + CH_3COOH + NAD$$

— a mnemonic that somehow escapes me whenever a bottle of gin heaves into sight.

People do go on about one's liver, but what about spontaneous combustion, eh? Dickens is more alarming than all those California doctors put together, if one recalls the fate of Mr Krook, Lord Chancellor of the Rag and Bottle shop in *Bleak House*, 'continually in liquor', of whom nothing is left after a carouse too many save a 'smouldering vapour in the room, and a dark greasy coating on the walls and ceiling...call the death by any name...it is the same death eternally — inborn, inbred, engendered in the corrupted humours of the vicious body itself, and that only – Spontaneous Combustion, and none other of all the deaths that can be died.'

It turns the stomach – pass the brandy...

Let us topers turn to happier happenings. Tokay Essenz is made in the far north-east of Hungary, from grapes that have been shrivelled into concentrated sweetness by the 'noble rot' that also informs such great sauternes as Yquem, individually picked and allowed to let drip their juice, without being pressed, but simply under their own weight. This clear, golden, intensely honey-sweet wine is credited with all sorts of therapeutic, not to mention aphrodisiac, qualities. It is said indeed that, applied to the lips of a dying man, it will restore him to life.

In my modest cellar there is a half-litre bottle apiece for my wife, my son and me, against our respective appointed days – not that we believe in these old babushkas' tales but in the pure spirit of scientific curiosity. So it was with Raymond Postgate, as sceptical as a man could be, but who bade his family have a bottle handy, and let's see... When, with the end nigh, the wine was duly applied, he did not, alas, come back to life but, the family later told me, he died not only with the Tokay Essenz on his lips, but with a smile.

The learned Mrs M.F.K. Fisher, the Elizabeth David of the United

States, in her little book, *A Cordiall Water*, 'a garland of odd and old receipts to assuage the ills of man and beast', recommended 'gin for women's monthly misery. "Gin is our best friend, girl," a fellow sufferer informed me soberly in a coal town in southern Illinois. "It's not the liquor in it, it's the juniper juice that does the trick."'

But among what she calls her 'cure-alls', suitable for both sexes and all ages, 'the simplest of all,' she says, 'and the most all-embracing, is what in France is called "a little slice of ham"...which, especially when taken in bed with a glass of good wine, will cure completely or at least help cure exhaustion, migraine, *grippe*, gout, disappointment in love, business worries, childbed fever, dizziness, coughing, and indeed almost everything else except Death and Taxes.'

People who follow this prescription, says Mrs Fisher, 'will not suffer from indigestion. Their livers will not shrivel in one last paroxysm of revulsion before the dainty fat slice of embalmed porkflesh, and the salted pickles, and the mildly alcoholic flushing of the fermented grape juice. They will not, in other words, die. *Then*.'

There are those, I know, who keep brandy in the house purely for medicinal reasons, and very sensible, too. Vyvyan Holland, who survived the cruel indignities he suffered as a child for being the son of Oscar Wilde to become the kindest and most civilized of men, once told me of a great-uncle who used to keep a few rare bottles of fine old cognac for special friends.

Came a day when his house took fire, and one particular fireman behaved with exceptional courage. The old gentleman offered him a glass of his oldest and finest in grateful tribute, upon which the fireman, drenched by the hoses, took off boots and socks, saying, 'A very happy thought, sir, and thank you kindly. I'm a teetotaller myself, but there's nothing like brandy for stopping a cold,' and poured the golden glory over his feet.

Punch: Food and Booze Extra,
July 1985

Two Harvests in Tuscany

Elizabeth Romer

October: Vintage

O RLANDO sniffs the air anxiously now, on the clear starlit nights. He is secretly willing away the first light frosts so that he can gather in all of his tobacco crop before the glittering crystals destroy the remaining tall plants. Already the leaves of the cherry and pear trees have turned colour and been whisked off the branches by brisk winds. The hillsides are stippled with gold and the skies are cold blue. For the past week or so all around the valley the farmers and ordinary householders who have a few vines around their houses have been cleaning their barrels and fetching out their *follatore*, the grape crushing machines. The grapes are ripe, as plump and sweet as they can be expected to be, and on the first day when the tobacco kilns are full and no more can be gathered, Orlando judges that the *vendemmia* can begin. The moon is in the right phase, on the wane, so they can pick the grapes with easy minds.

Silvana enjoys the *vendemmia* and always arranges her work so that she too may join in the picking. At six-thirty in the morning Orlando drives the large tractor down the hill to the fields below. On the trailer behind are stacked large square containers and a heap of baskets. Silvana and her friend Nena are perched among the baskets and following along behind come Menchino, round like a *putto*, and blond with bright blue eyes, and Guido's twin brothers Tonio and Alfredo, whose dark bobbed hair makes them look like a couple of Renaissance pages. They are all armed with iron clippers in the shape of secateurs, some with curved handles that cradle the fist. Most of their baskets are of brightly coloured plastic, large and oval with one deep handle. However Silvana has a real twig basket made for her by an elderly relative who still makes the *canestre* in the long winter evenings. This craft dates back to Roman times, when it was advocated by Cato as a seemly activity to keep the farm workers busy on cold winter nights. Silvana's basket is a curious shape. Its handle is cut from a branch with four prongs, two of which make the curved handle. The two smaller branches are left and trimmed off to make small projections that can be conveniently used to hang the basket from the vine, so leaving the two hands free for picking; the body is made from woven twigs. As soon as the basket is full it can be emptied into the large wooden cases and plastic containers and the whole process started again.

Silvana works next to Nena, both of them neatly and quickly stripping the vines, laughing and talking all the while as they cut the bunches easily with sharp clippers. They work carefully, not tearing away at the boughs, which will be left to die back until it is time for Guido to prune them again next March or April. As the day wears on they move to the higher fields which are smaller and are planted in the antique manner with pergolas holding good quality grapes. They group themselves in fours and fives working together around one large arbour, bending and stretching amongst the livid gold leaves and blue-black grapes as on some animated Attic freeze. The cases of grapes become fuller and fuller, mountains of fruit, green and black, covered with bloom and oozing juice from their own weight. The pickers' hands are sticky and there is a heavy scent of fruit in the warming air. The men discard their darned woollen jumpers and their muscles strain under their faded shirts. Nena and Silvana, both by now bare-armed, take care not to get stung by the nettles or torn by the odd bramble that winds itself around the roots of the vines. The vines are too many and the labourers too few to spend time cleaning around each plant, and so in the further fields the grapes flourish among hedgerows choked with field flowers, stray corn and tall grasses. They stumble on a hide made by some passing hunter. The once green leaves of the broken branches are withered and brown, the trodden ground littered with spent cartridges. Orlando mutters under his breath about thieving hunters. Silvana wants to keep some of the grapes apart for eating. Tonio reaches for the most luxuriant bunches and cuts them off with a T-shaped piece of the hard vine still attached so that she can hang the clusters from the nails in the storeroom beams. These will keep well until December.

They halt for a break and sprawl themselves in the shade of a large arbour, the sun playing through the leaves on to their red flushed faces. Silvana passes around the flasks of last year's wine and Orlando drinks from the bottle, the wine trickling down his broad chin and staining his shirt a dull pink. Andrea is perched on the edge of the group, his shirt tied in the fashion of fifteen years ago in a knot under his belly, exposing a vast expanse of grubby woollen vest. His three dogs have followed the progress of the pickers and, as soon as they move on, the animals root and sniff at the base of the stripped vines, searching for and eating the grapes that drop to the ground and escape the baskets. Silvana says that they eat the fallen figs too and every day they come around to the fig tree. So do the foxes, says Nena, and they steal the grapes from the vine, she has seen them. But she says this is better luck for the chickens: the foxes are less likely to rob the hen coops when there is fruit on the vine. Orlando, interested in the conversation, says that he has heard from a professor in Cortona that in the very old days, the Roman *contadini* would fatten young foxes on grapes and eat them. There is a general groan of disgust at this piece of information. Even in the worst years of the war they had not sunk to such unappetizing depths.

After they have gathered the last grape and the cases are loaded on to the trailer, the black and green grapes always kept separate, they all make their way back to the *fattoria*. The day's grape gathering has nothing to do with the greater world of wine, vintages, labels and commerce. This is simply a group of country people, timeless in their attitudes and expressions, and as their forefathers did, they have gathered in the fruits of their labours. After all the ancient Greeks' name for the Italian peninsula was Oenotria, the land of wine.

Now they set to to make the wine that is as necessary to their lives as bread and water. Behind the chapel and down a slope under some walnut trees is the *cantina*, the cellar, which is long and cool with a shallowly vaulted ceiling. Here the grapes are pressed and the wine kept in the huge oak barrels that line the walls. The tractor is driven round to the *cantina* and the cases unloaded, and the pressing of the grapes begins immediately. It is already dusk and the men work on into the night. The long room is lit by two dim light-bulbs dangling on dusty wires from the crumbling bricks, the walls are encrusted with aged dust and the cobwebbed barrels are immense in the shadows. The three men, Guido, Menchino and Tonio, watched by Sauro, move in the gloom operating the machinery like warlocks in some vast devil's kitchen. The shadows on their faces deepen in the faint light and if it were not for their clothes it would be difficult to put a date to the scene.

First they tip the cases of green grapes into a funnel-shaped apparatus outside the *cantina* wall, then they turn a handle like that of a mangle at the base of the funnel which half presses the fruit and sends the liquid and skins cascading through a window into a deep-walled stone trough inside the *cantina*. Here Tonio stirs the must with a long pole and rakes over the skins. This funnel-shaped machine, the *follatore*, is a simple form of the *égrappoir*, the machine used for the same purpose in more elaborate vineyards. The Cerottis' version has however no refinement to remove the stalks from the grapes, it is just a simple crushing device. The juice or must is filtered from the stone trough into the wooden vats through a large plastic pipe, the liquid sent on its way by a hand pump. The skins are then put into presses shaped like barrels with open slatted sides. A screw is turned at the top and this forces a plate down on to the skins, squeezing the remaining juice out between the side slats. A turgid yellow-green froth bubbles sluggishly from the base of the presses. This press wine, which is strong and full of tannin from the skins, is later added to the must in the fermenting barrels. The wrung-out skins, which some farmers use to make a rough *grappa*, in much the same way as French farmers make *marc*, are finally thrown out on to a field well away from the house as they would harm any poultry that ventured to eat them.

The black grapes are crushed in a separate machine and their must is put into an oak barrel together with the skins. The longer the skins are left in the darker the wine will be. The wine will clarify, the sugar turning into alcohol, in about ten days' time, but the vats will remain unsealed for about a month in order to complete the fermentation. When this happens the barrels will be sealed properly with an air-tight clay seal to prevent the alcohol content of the wine dissipating and the wine turning to vinegar.

Back at the house the kitchen is rosy red from the huge log fire. Orlando hangs a long square blackened tin from the hook on the chimney chain ready to boil up some fresh chestnuts. This month is the time when the ripe heavy brown nuts fall from the tall trees and Sauro has been industriously collecting them by the sackful to store in one of the upper attics so that they may enjoy roasting them during the coming winter. Everyone gathers around the fire, drinking wine and eating the nuts which, being so fresh, have milk-white soft flesh. The skins they save for the animals, as Silvana sees to it that nothing is wasted in the household. The men have washed away the juice of the grapes and combed their hair ready for the supper which everyone will eat together in celebration of a successful day. Nena, clean and neat in a new pinafore, her hair covered with a spotted scarf, is helping Silvana. She lays a white cloth on the long wooden table, then places the glasses, plates, bowls and cutlery, three huge crusty loaves of bread, massive bowls of fruit and walnuts and the last of the old wine.

Meanwhile Silvana is cooking the supper. She makes two dishes of *funghi* cooked *in umido*, one of *porcini* flavoured with garlic and *mentuccia* and the other of *guatelli*, chanterelles, flavoured with parsley. There is also a large *frittata di cipollo*, an onion-flavoured omelette, country sausages grilled with sage leaves over the fire, and after walnuts and one of the last soft fruits of the year that ripen during this month, the *cachi*, the beautiful vermilion-coloured Japanese persimmons. Sauro picks the fruit from the tall, elegantly shaped tree at the end of the kitchen garden. When the leaves have fallen the tree looks spectacular with its large round glowing fruit hanging on the bare silver-grey branches. Eventually the food is ready and everyone takes his place at the table. By this time they are all hungry and enjoy the spicy butcher's sausages crisp from the fire and the succulent mushrooms with their rich sauce that everyone mops up with the fresh bread.

✳   ✳   ✳

After the meal is finished Orlando decides to make some hot spiced wine. He reaches for a small cauldron and fills it with three or four litres of red wine. Meanwhile Silvana has been sent to the *dispensa* to fetch some cinnamon sticks, cloves, an orange, a lemon and a bag of sugar. She also brings a bottle of brandy from the *tinello* in the dining room. Orlando tips a generous measure of sugar into the wine, then breaks a few cinnamon sticks and scatters in the fragments. He adds a few of the *chiodi di garofani*, the cloves, and some lemon and orange peel which he pares off with his pocket knife. Then the cauldron is slung over the fire to heat while Orlando watches to see that it does not boil and lose its alcohol. The last ingredient to go in is a big glass or two of brandy.

Orlando is in an expansive mood, well pleased with his year's harvests and ready to talk and relax a little. When the wine is hot enough he ladles it out into the toughened glass wine glasses which are the traditional trumpet shaped type, to be seen in any country bar and in most country kitchens. He and his men laugh and talk on, their faces becoming more animated and their voices louder with the conversation and the hot wine. They are feeling their masculinity, asserting their opinions, sure of their worth and their own importance, displaying the confidence that has been instilled into them with their mother's milk, products of a religion that worships the Boy Child. The fire dies down and Silvana sits at the end of the table, her head propped in her hand, trying to keep her eyes from closing. At last, aware that the next day begins at six, the men cease their talk, heave on their coats and start out into the cold night air to their homes. Orlando pokes his nose outside the door and is happy that he cannot smell any frost in the air.

December: Olive Harvest

DECEMBER is the month when Orlando usually chooses to gather his olives, although many gather theirs in November and even in late October. It all depends on the area and on the extent of ripeness that the farmer wants from his crop. Some olives are picked when they are immature and green and are preserved in brine, others are left until they are a strange, almost porphyry-purple colour. This the state in which, although the olive is not completely ripe, it is more nutritious and will make more deliciously flavoured oil. The berries become a shiny black when they are totally ripe.

There are two basic methods of collecting the olives. Some farmers prefer to spread nets under the trees and allow the ripe olives to drop into them. This method is obviously not labour-intensive but the olives gathered in this manner do not make the best oil. Orlando and Silvana prefer the old-fashioned, finger-numbing method of gathering the olives by hand. Silvana excavates the old olive baskets from a corner of the attic. These baskets are of a very particular apron-like shape; constructed of small branches and osiers, they are flat on one side and curved in a semi-circular bowl on the other. The flat side is held against the stomach with the aid of the gatherer's belt and a wooden catch. The semi-circular basket sticks out in front ready to receive the olives; in this way both the hands are left free for picking. The men, each with a basket slung at his waist, climb up to the grove on the terraced slope above the *fattoria*, taking a couple of rough wooden ladders to reach to the tops of the gnarled old trees. After all the olives are picked, Orlando will take them to Cortona to the *frantoia* where they will be pressed, then he will bring back the oil to be stored in large pottery jars in the ground-floor storeroom next to the pantry. One hundred kilos of oil will be sufficient to last the household for about a year.

The best quality olive oil comes from olives that are hand-picked before they are completely ripe and black, and the oil must be the product of the first pressing in a cold press, that is, ground between stones in the old-fashioned way and not in a machine. This is called *Olio di Prima Spremitura*; it is pure olive oil, unaffected by heat and is the most flavourful and easily digestible of all cooking oils. It is also extremely expensive and not easily found in normal shops even in Italy. However some of the most superior food stores in the large towns and cities do sell this oil; very often it comes from the olive groves of famous vineyards and wine producers. Its good flavour somewhat depends on the type of soil and the area in which the olive is grown and the test of its purity is that it contains 1% or less of oleic acid.

There are several grades of olive oil and they are again distinguished by the percentage of acid they contain. *Olio Extravergine d'Oliva*, the best olive oil that is available normally, contains not more than 1% oleic acid. *Olio Sopraffino Vergine d'Oliva* has not more than 1.5%, then there is *Olio, Fino Vergine d'Oliva* with 3% and, finally, *Olio Vergine d'Oliva* with not more than 4% acid content. Obviously the *Extravergine* will have the best flavour; it will be the most expensive, but is the most excellent and flavoursome oil to pour over a salad or on to a hot vegetable. The cheaper olive oils are splendidly adequate for frying and other forms of cooking.

The yield of oil from a *quintale* of olives, that is 100 kilos, is a source of much discussion. Some farmers claim as much as 16 kilos for every 100 kilos of berries, others insist that nine is more usual. About ten to twelve is probably the average, though much depends on the quality of the olives themselves and the soil on which they are grown. In one exceptional year Orlando obtained 19 kilos per 100 and was delighted. Italians are fiercely partisan about the quality and flavour of their oils. Lucca in the north of Tuscany claims to have the best oil in Italy, a claim hotly disputed by southerners who say their oil is the richest and best. Personally I find that the green oil from the hills around Florence has the truest, sweetest, most fruity flavour of all, though the Aretini would not agree. In short the Italians prefer their own. Silvana certainly does; in her opinion olive oil bought from shops and coming from other parts of Italy is a suspect substance. She knows her own oil contains nothing but good olives. Choosing oil therefore remains a question of personal taste.

When buying olive oil it is worth remembering the different grades of oil and to go for an *Olio Extravergine d'Oliva* if possible. The greener and darker the oil, the fruitier and more flavourful it is likely to be. Avoid pale yellowish Italian olive oil as it can be too refined, with a resulting loss of flavour. Price, too, is a good guide: the best is usually the most expensive.

Olive oil belongs to the warm Mediterranean. It complements the fiery flavours of garlic and peppers and the oily aromatic wild oregano that are used in Provence, Spain and Greece. Although there is a belt of butter based cooking in its northern regions, Italy firmly belongs to the list of countries cooking in the Mediterranean way. Tuscan food depends upon oil. Bread and olive oil together are a foundation of Tuscan cooking and this is well demonstrated by the numerous olive groves that cover the landscape. Olive oil is another of the basic ingredients that is always in copious supply in Silvana's kitchen and which gives her cooking its character. She of course uses it in nearly all her cookery from salads, roasts and grills, and dishes cooked *in umido* right through to soups. The only things for which she will select a lighter oil are deep-fried *polpette* or vegetables coated in flour and egg and sweet fried cakes. For these she uses an arachide oil or one made from mixed vegetable oils. However when she wants the dish to be extra delicious she will use olive oil, as in years gone by when everything was cooked in olive oil.

✻   ✻   ✻

Orlando and Silvana keep their olive oil in large pottery jars and straw-covered glass demi-johns that have wide necks. The jars must be very carefully sealed with heavy lids or tight-fitting corks. This precaution is taken because mice love olive oil. If they can dislodge a lid they will climb into the jars and naturally they cannot get out again; this means that the whole jar containing twenty-eight litres will be spoilt. Silvana says that this disaster befell her family during the war and that the polluted oil could not even be used to light the little pottery lamps that they burned with old oil as fuel and a scrap of cotton as a wick.

December is of course the great month for entertaining. Festivities seem to start on the Sunday before Christmas and extend to Epiphany. On this Sunday, Silvana's brother Paulo, her sister-in-law Anna and their young son Roberto are expected from Castiglion

Fiorentino for a family lunch. Silvana loves to have company as an excuse to cook a special meal and she enjoys hearing all the family news. She gets up early to make some fresh *tagliatelle*. Silvana uses the traditional recipe for making the pasta, using six eggs to one kilo or two and a half pounds of flour. Normal *pastasciutta* like spaghetti is not made with eggs but the home-made pastas and the ribbon pastas bought from the stores are often enriched with egg and this gives them a different flavour and texture. She heaps the flour on to the scrubbed pantry table and into a well in the middle she breaks the eggs; she mixes these ingredients if necessary with a little water into a firm dough. Strictly speaking the dough should then be rolled out on an enormous board or table with a very long rolling pin, one metre in length and made of wood. The dough is rolled very thinly, then rolled again until it is almost transparent; by then it hangs down the edges of the table like a tablecloth. This takes an exact texture of dough and years of experience to achieve. Next, the sheet must be rolled into a loose swiss roll shape and then, using a very sharp long knife, the roll is cut into thin slices the size of wide baby ribbon; this is the *tagliatelle*. *Tagliarini* is cut into finer strips and *pappardelle*, a favourite in Arezzo, into ribbons half an inch wide. The coils of pasta are then left to rest a while before being plunged into turbulently boiling water for the brief cooking that fresh pasta requires. It needs space, time and practice to make *tagliatelle* in this manner, so many housewives have a pasta machine like a small mangle into which they can feed already rolled out sheets of dough to achieve the required exquisite fineness.

The fine sheets are then put through a second set of rollers which cut the pasta into ribbons. Silvana uses one of these little old-fashioned machines which she has had since her marriage. She normally only makes fresh pasta for guests and family Sunday lunches. For every day, when there may be twenty or more people to feed, she uses ordinary pasta bought in vast quantities from the village shop.

As the cauldron of boiling water bubbles over the fire ready to receive the *tagliatelle*, Silvana bastes the chicken grilling on a trivet and stews some pieces of pork fillet in a pan with white wine, sage and garlic. With the chicken liver she intends to make one of her *crostini* recipes. She mashes the previously poached livers into about four ounces of softened butter to make a smooth pomade seasoned with salt and black pepper, then spreads the mixture onto thin small rounds of bread. To add variety she mixes some more butter with anchovy paste and again spreads it on more rounds of the white Tuscan bread, topping each piece with a fat caper that she has pickled herself in their own wine vinegar.

*   *   *

In Tuscany and Umbria most families eat *tortellini* at Christmas, especially on Christmas Eve. They also eat it all the year round but Christmas time is the traditional time to eat the filled pasta. Perhaps this also dates back to the period when people spiced the bread to make it special and maybe, in the same way, enlivened their basic pasta with a filling to make it rich and festive. The small cushions of pasta have different names in diverse parts of Italy, different shapes and different fillings. *Tortellini* can also be called *tortelloni*, if they are very large, sometimes they are known as *cappelletti* or *agnolotti* and sometimes as *ravioli*; this is not such a common name as might be supposed, although it is well known in Britain in the form of the tinned variety, which bears absolutely no relationship to the real thing. Ravioli is usually filled with a mixture of ricotta cheese, a mild soft sheep's cheese, and very finely chopped spinach or *bietole*, spinach beet. It is normally served with butter, a sage leaf or two and some parmesan sprinkled over the surface. The other filled pastas, the *tortellini* and the *capelletti*, are usually filled with some sort of meat mixture: either a mixture of lean veal and pork ground very very fine, spiced with parmesan, garlic and parsley or possibly ground beef mixed maybe with *mortadella*, flavoured with rosemary, bound with red wine, enriched with parmesan and nutmeg. There are many varieties in these fillings and the pasta is usually served in a bowl of well-flavoured bouillon.

*   *   *

Silvana's favourite filling is of chicken breast shredded and pounded very fine, garlic minutely minced, parsley, parmesan cheese, salt, pepper and nutmeg, the ingredients bound together into a smooth tight paste with an egg. To make her *tortellini* she uses the same dough as for her *tagliatelle* but in this case cuts out rounds of fine dough with a small circular scalloped pastry cutter. On half of the circle she places a small spoon of filling then she folds the pasta over to make a semi-circle, moistening the edges and firmly pressing

191

them down. The *ravioli* are generally square in shape and the *tortellini* and *cappelletti* can be made by folding a square over diagonally with the stuffing inside the triangle produced, then by taking the corners of the triangle and drawing them together to form a small ring. Legend has it that one night Venus stayed at an inn in central Italy. The cook, beguiled by her beauty, stared in at her while she slept; he was so overcome with the shape of her navel that he invented *tortellini* in honour of it. Indeed these small round folded bonne-bouches are rather reminiscent in shape of belly buttons. Of course they are exceptionally good when served simply with butter and some slices of truffle, especially the cheese-filled *ravioli*. In Torino it is possible to eat the subtlest and most delicious kinds of *ravioli*, sometimes filled with delicate mixtures of salt water fish, finished in sauces of butter and pine kernels, which add an interesting texture to the soft *ravioli*, or filled with *fonduta*, the rich mixture of melted cheeses that is a triumph of Italian culinary art.

✳   ✳   ✳

On Christmas day Orlando, Silvana and Sauro will usually have a quiet lunch together, enjoying the special dishes such as the *faraona in salmi* and the *filetto di tacchino*. They will exchange gifts; this is the time when Sauro will be given a new bicycle, or some such important present. But on the whole Christmas for the Cerottis is not the extravagant gift-giving celebration that it is elsewhere – Silvana and Orlando appreciate a quiet day in their otherwise crowded year. Later in the day they may go visiting or receive relatives.

Over the long holiday period the *fattoria* will be full of guests for lunch and dinner. Silvana will certainly serve the *cardi* in one of its forms. Just as certainly the *tinello* in the long dining room will be laden with piles of sweet home-made biscuits, bowls of walnuts, clementines and dried figs. There will be several large *pannettone*, some filled with candied fruit and some with small pieces of bitter chocolate embedded in the light sponge. Silvana will also serve the delicious *zabajone* when the spirits flag and delicate glasses of *vin santo* to moisten the almond biscuits. Orlando will open an impressive number of bottles of *spumante d'Asti* to toast their guests and all the friends who will drop in to wish them well for the new year that is dawning.

The Tuscan Year, 1984

Two Brandies:
Two Countries

Elizabeth Ray

L EAVE Cognac, where the famous brandy comes from, after breakfast, and by lunchtime you will be in the heart of the Armagnac country, home of the other great grape brandy. There are vines all the way, for as the Cognac vineyards come to an end there are those of Pomerol, in the claret country, to fill the gap before the rolling vine-clad hills of Armagnac come into sight.

A mere three hours' drive, but countries far apart in feeling. The Armagnac landscape is rougher, the houses poorer and the food richer than those in the Charentes – the region of which the town of Cognac is spiritually (in more senses than one) the capital city. There is no town named Armagnac – the name is that of a region, and that of a spirit, and of a spirit that is not only a great brandy but also the tradition and the feeling of Gascony, which bred such vigorous, exuberant creatures as d'Artagnan and the Three Musketeers. The Charentais, although such near neighbours, call themselves *cagouillards*, after the local snails: their way of life is gentler and slower. Their landscape is green and white; the river Charente flows slowly through the woods, the meadows and the vineyards; cows, all white or black and white, browse as slowly in green fields; the chalky soil is pale and so are the houses; for most of the year the vines, stretching into the distance, are green, too; and the light seems pearly. Gascony is golden, a land as much of the grain as the grape, for the fields of maize mass the roadsides even more closely than the vines. The soil is sand or clay, rich in colour, the cattle golden to match. When I was last there, in the autumn, trees and vines were red and gold, and the low sun bathed everything in a golden glow.

Here and there, it is true, the landscape can look deceptively English. Hills and trees are similar and sometimes there are bramble bushes along the roads, heavy with blackberries, where usually there are vines or maize. Look at the houses, though, stone or half-timbered, with heavy wooden shutters and low-pitched roofs, tiled with terracotta, and you realize that this is not only France, but southern France, though not so far south that there are olives. This is goose-fat country, just as the nearby Charentes is butter-cooking country, and Provence, no further away to the east, cooks in olive oil. It is one of the fascinations of France that so small a country offers such varieties of cooking and of culture. The forests of the Landes, overlapping the vine-growing area, teem with wild boar, deer, pheasant and pigeon; the farms of the more open country are alive with the geese and the ducks that are reared and fattened for the *foie gras* and the *magrets*, fillets of duck breast, that are so special to the region.

Both the cognac and the armagnac countries lie on the pilgrims' way to Santiago di Compostella in Spain, and each has early Romanesque churches, grand and important such as the one in Aulnay, near St Jean d'Angély, or tiny like the one near Cazaubon, with no village anywhere near, yet not forgotten, for it is still in occasional use. Gascony is rich, too, as is the Dordogne, in the *bastide* towns of the Hundred Years War, built in a geometric pattern for easy defence – this south-western corner of France owed allegiance to the English crown and was fought over as the tide of battle ebbed and flowed. La Bastide d'Armagnac (the only town or village I came across with 'Armagnac' actually in its name) is a lovely example.

The tiny town, in the Bas Armagnac region, where the finest brandies come from, has an exquisite central square, the church forming one side, the others arcaded and half-timbered, their small shops discreetly hidden, their upper stories with flowered window-boxes. A long-handled water pump stands in one corner, and there are no 'attractions' for tourists, not even a picture-postcard shop. It is quiet, unspoiled, and not in the least self-conscious about it, even though Henri IV once stayed here, and took the square as model for the elegant Place des Vosges in Paris.

The Mayor of Bastide, Monsieur Loubert, has a distillery just outside the town, where he distils for the large (by Armagnac standards) firm of Chabot, as well as for small growers. The Chabot *chai* is nearby, recognizable by the black fungus growing on its walls, caused by the slow evaporation of the spirit maturing in casks within, as it does in Cognac.

It is as unrealistic to compare the two brandies as it is to compare claret and burgundy: each is distinguished, both are different. Armagnac has probably a longer history, but cognac is far better-known – production is ten times as great, export perhaps proportionately even greater. In Cognac they refer kindly to armagnac as 'our little cousin'. The grapes for both brandies are the same, and although until recently armagnac was matured in casks of the black local oak, much is now aged in the same lighter Limousin or Tronçais oak as cognac. The difference in character arises from the soils – chalk for cognac, clay or sand for armagnac – and from the methods of distillation: armagnac is distilled once to cognac's twice, and at a lower temperature, retaining more of the original flavouring elements. Thus armagnac is racier of the soil, cognac subtler, but neither is superior to the other: choice between them is a subjective matter. It may well be, too, that Gascony's warmer climate is reflected in the style of armagnac, as in the southern liveliness of its people. Cognac is the home of immensely big firms, such as Martell, Hennessy and Camus; armagnac is still made by small growers and sold direct to the shippers, though Janneau in Condom and Chabot in Villeneuve de Marsan account for a good deal of export.

I reached the armagnac region the day that picking began, finding that as in many wine-growing areas today, it is done more and more by machine, grudgingly accepted here as an economic necessity, but not much loved by the Gascons, proud of their traditions. Monsieur Dufau, Chabot's master *vigneron*, pulled a face when he told me that it wasn't so much the machine that he minded, but that so few people are now involved in the vintage – the machine does as much in fifteen days as forty people used to do in a month. 'We work all the year for this day,' he said, 'and it used to be a time of fun and friendship for lots of people. Now, look – there are only four of us: one to drive the machine, one to take the grapes to the press, one to look after the press, and myself to keep an eye on it all.' The cumbersome machines straddle the vines, shaking the grapes loose from their stalks with surprising delicacy and vibrating them on to a conveyor-belt that takes them to a container at the top of the tractor, which is then emptied into a waiting truck. More and more vineyards are now planted specially to accommodate the machines – the vines further apart than of old, and trained higher from the ground, so that the flippers that shake the grapes loose can reach them all. In those vineyards still unprepared some grapes are left behind, and must be gleaned by hand.

Many wine-growing regions make a sweet aperitif by stopping fermentation with spirit. Cognac's *pineau* is probably the best and best-known: the armagnac version is *floc*, widely sold locally, and more like the *ratafia* of Champagne – any of them goes well in a scooped-out melon, or served with ice-cream. Compared with the others, *floc* is a fairly new product, and Monsieur Dufau, typical Gascon conservative, pulled another of his expressive faces when I asked him about it. 'Not traditional,' he said, and that was that. Much nicer, to my taste, are a Belle Sandrine, a delicious blend of armagnac and passion-fruit juice that makes a richly fragrant sweet liqueur, and the fruits conserved in a syrup of armagnac and sugar, to be eaten as a dessert. Gerland, a firm that produces armagnac only for the French market, makes these confections of cherries, plums from nearby Agen and – the one I like best – Mirabelle plums.

The Gascons are very close to the soil and live, in consequence, as well as any people in France, growing or rearing much of their own food – one farm we visited was completely self-sufficient except for bread (which *maman* could have baked had she had a mind to it, and didn't need the excuse to bicycle into the village to pick up all the local gossip at the baker's). The family lived off its own vegetables, eggs, poultry, pigs, their own wine, and game shot locally.

They are sportsmen, too. A small church near La Bastide d'Armagnac is dedicated to cyclists, who pray there for success, and give votive offerings of their winning shirts or bicycles; many towns have an area for the Course Landaise – a regional form of bull-fighting – and its own team for the Course, held every week throughout the summer. These fights, peculiar to the region, differ from other forms of bull-fighting in that they are not meant to kill the bull, or the man either (there are no horses) but to demonstrate courage and skill. The bull is held on a long rope by one member of the team while the *ecarteur* makes his passes at it, so that if he is in real danger the bull can be checked; the couple or so of *sauteurs* make amazingly last-minute leaps over the angry beast, and a jury awards points: there is handsome prize money to the winning team in the grand final at the end of the season.

*   *   *   *

They say that in every restaurant in Paris you will find a Gascon – perhaps in the kitchen, perhaps as a waiter, but someone somewhere, for every Gascon cares about food. In Gascony, towns are small and far apart; there are few sophisticated amusements, and home entertaining is important, so that every Gasconne is a good cook, and friendly rivalry obtains as to who, for instance, makes the best *pastis* – not a sort of absinthe, but a thin pastry, rather like the Greek *filo*, stuffed with fruit soaked in armagnac.

Especially, the men like to shoot. The great pine forests of the Landes abound in a wide variety of game, but the Gascon waits impatiently for the arrival of the *palombe*, the wild dove. Every year, usually on St Luke's Day, which often coincides with the opening of the vintage, the *palombes* begin to pass over the Landes, as they migrate south, and a strange epidemic afflicts the men – *palombite*, or what we could call palombitis. Shops put up their shutters, restaurants close, the post is delayed and the village streets are deserted: the men are at the *palombières*. These are well-constructed hides, half above, half below ground, camouflaged with bracken and – the one I was in, at any rate – as spacious and well-appointed as Mr Badger's house, with a cosy kitchen and room for a dozen people to sit down to a meal, with another half-dozen watching for the birds.

The idea is to attract the migrating birds by using decoy pigeons, specially kept for the job. They are hooded, not to be distracted, and are put high into trees on wooden perches attached by wires to the *palombière*. As soon as birds are sighted the wires are pulled slightly so that the perches move and the decoys flap their wings to keep their balance, thus encouraging the migrants to feel that this must be a good resting place. Lured to the ground, they are netted if they are many, shot if they are few. Every day until the end of November the *palombières* are filled with hopeful shots and their families and friends, some always on duty, coo-cooing to attract the birds, though from the ones I heard I doubt if they would have fooled any sensible *palombe*.

Shooting is not the only end in view; this is also a time for fellowship and good food, for this is Gascony, after all. On my one day in a *palombière* one of the local restaurateurs had closed for the week (another one's turn next week) bringing not only his culinary skills from the Relais de la Haute Lande in Luxey but also his head waiter, another keen small-game hunter. Lunch began with oysters, followed by hot whole *foie gras* with apples, then *magrets* of duck grilled over a wood fire in the kitchen. Readers must forgive me if I cannot recall what came between the aperitif, a glass of new sauternes from the nearby Bordelais, not yet fully fermented, and the enormous cake that rounded off the picnic, decorated with autumn leaves and icing-sugar squirrels, brought by the local *patissier*, who had also shut up shop for the week. The eating was better than the shooting – the day's bag was one *palombe*.

But other birds loom large in these parts, for this is *foie gras* country, with geese and ducks being fattened for their livers on the maize that grows so abundantly here, where it is a common sight to see the large 'cribs' crammed with cobs for winter use. St Sever, between Bordeaux and Pau, in the district known as La Chalosse, is a town almost entirely given up – save for the arena for the Course Landaise – to the rearing, fattening and processing of the birds.

I visited one of the local farms to see dignified and stately Toulouse geese and the more flibberty ducks, dashing wildly around. These are a special breed called *mulard*, a cross between the Pekin and the Barbary, which grows to twice the size of a roasting bird. The birds range freely until about six weeks old, when they are taken indoors to be maize-fed and fattened for another two or three weeks; the geese are fed three times a day, the ducks twice. It used to be a hand operation, with the goose-handler forcing the food down the birds' throats through a funnel, but now the food goes in through a machine, rather like a milking machine in reverse, but the principle is the same. Each bird is individually fed until it can no longer walk. Of course, I had my doubts about the humanity or otherwise of the process, but I must admit that the birds seemed quite happy about their lot, coming eagerly to meet us as we approached at the appointed time. This particular farm belongs to the Tastet family, four generations all engaged, with 700 geese and 3000 ducks to look after on their 50-acre farm, being bred and fed for the firm of Sarrade in St Sever, where it was impressive to see the speed and skill with which the birds are dealt with, the products packed and despatched by refrigerated lorries to reach Paris and Brussels the next morning.

Nothing is wasted. The liver is the best-known and the most highly prized part, but the meat of geese and ducks is made into *confits* – the pieces salted and then cooked in their own fat, which preserves them for months, to form the basis for dishes such as *cassoulet*. Duck breasts are cut into *magrets*, so important in *cuisine nouvelle* and the like, sometimes served fresh as a hot dish, sometimes smoked and served thinly sliced in a *salade Landaise*. Neck meat and giblets are often served *en brochette*, and feathers and down are sold to a bedding factory.

There are many grades of *foie gras*. The finest and most expensive is the whole liver, such as we had at the *palombière*, delicate but rich. The factory sends it fresh and vacuum-packed for immediate despatch, to be used within ten days, or in tins for longer life. The *bloc* of pâté, with a truffle embedded in its middle, is better-known and packed in various sizes of tin, priced accordingly, and there are *crèmes* and *mousses* in tins that have other liver mixed with that of goose or duck, and that much cheaper.

All this from Gascony, a country with games to play, game to eat, a benign climate, proud people and good armagnac to drink. All this and *foie gras* too – one can almost hear Sydney Smith's sound of trumpets...

BREAKFASTS AND BREAKFASTS

'There are breakfasts and breakfasts'
George Augustus Sala

'A Scanty Fork Breakfast'

Mr Jorrocks Entertains a Fellow
Fox-Hunter

R. S. Surtees

ABOUT a yard and a half from the fire was placed the breakfast-table; in the centre stood a magnificent uncut ham, with a great quartern loaf on one side, a huge Bologna sausage on the other; besides these there were nine eggs, two pyramids of muffins, a great deal of toast, a dozen ship-biscuits, and half a pork-pie, while a dozen kidneys were spluttering on a spit before the fire, and Betsey held a gridiron covered with mutton-chops on the top; altogether there was as much as would have served ten people. 'Now sit down,' said Jorrocks, 'and let us be doing, for I am as hungry as a hunter. Hope you are *peckish* too; what shall I give you? tea or coffee?—but take both— coffee first and tea after a bit. If *I* can't give you them good, don't know who can. You must pay your *devours*, as we say in France, to the 'am, for it is an especial fine one, and *do* take a few eggs with it; there, I've not given you above a pound of 'am, but you can come again, you know— "waste not want not." Now take some muffins, *do*, pray. Betsey, bring some more cream, and set the kidneys on the table, the Yorkshireman is getting nothing to eat. Have a chop with your kidney, werry luxterous—I could eat an elephant stuffed with grenadiers, and wash them down with a ocean of tea; but pray lay in to the breakfast, or I shall think you don't like it. There, now take some tea and toast, or one of those biscuits, or whatever you like; would a little more 'am be agreeable? Betsey, run into the larder and see if your Missis left any of that cold chine of pork last night—and hear, bring the cold goose and any cold flesh you can lay hands on; there are really no wittles on the table. I am quite ashamed to set you down to such a scanty fork breakfast; but this is what comes of not being master of your own house. Hope your hat may long cover your family: rely upon it, it is "cheaper to buy your bacon than to keep a pig." ' Just as Jorrocks uttered these last words, the side door opened, and without either 'with your leave or by your leave,' in bounced Mrs Jorrocks in an elegant dishabille, with her hair tucked up in papers, and a pair of worsted slippers on her feet, worked with roses and blue lilies.

'Pray, *Mister* J.,' said she, 'what is the meaning of this card? I found it in your best coat pocket, which you had on last night, and I *do desire*, sir, that you will tell me how it came there. Goodmorning, sir (spying the Yorkshireman at last), perhaps *you* know where Mr Jorrocks was last night, and perhaps *you* can tell me who this person is whose card I have found in the corner of Mr Jorrocks's best coat pocket?' 'Indeed, madam,' replied the Yorkshireman, 'Mr Jorrocks's movements of yesterday evening are quite a secret to me. It is the night that he usually spends at the Magpie and Stump, but whether he was there or not I cannot pretend to say. As for the card, madam—' 'There, then, take it and read it,' interrupted Mrs J.; and he took the card accordingly—a delicate pale pink, with blue borders and gilt edge—and read—we would fain put all in dashes and asterisks—'Miss Juliana Granville, John-street, Waterloo-road.'

This digression giving Mr Jorrocks a moment or two to recollect himself, he pretended to get into a thundering passion, and seizing the card out of the Yorkshireman's hand, he thrust it into the fire, swearing it was an application for admission into the Deaf and Dumb Institution, where he wished he had Mrs J.

Mr Jorrocks's Jaunts and Jollities, 1830

Matter for a May Morning

Thomas Love Peacock

T HE divine took his seat at the breakfast-table, and began to compose his spirits by the gentle sedative of a large cup of tea, the demulcent of a well-buttered muffin, and the tonic of a small lobster.

The Rev Dr Folliott: You are a man of taste, Mr Crotchet. A man of taste is seen at once in the array of his breakfast-table. Chocolate, coffee, tea, cream, eggs, ham, tongue, cold fowl,—all these are good, and bespeak good knowledge in him who sets them forth: but the touchstone is fish: anchovy is the first step, prawns and shrimps the second; and I laud him who reaches even to these: potted char and lampreys are the third, and a fine stretch of progression; but lobster is, indeed, matter for a May morning, and demands a rare combination of knowledge and virtue in him who sets it forth.

Crotchet Castle, 1823

Awful Warning

George Augustus Sala

THERE are breakfasts and breakfasts; and it so happens that the bravest, the honestest, the truthfullest, and the most meat-eating peoples under the sun, the Germans and the Britons, with their transatlantic descendants and their Australasian brethren, are the only races who give the proper appellation to the first meal of the day. We break our fast at eight or nine a.m., and we rightly term that meal 'breakfast.' Quite as appropriately do the Teutons call their fracture of fast *Morgenbrod*. The Italians ought to say *rompere il digiuno*, when they take their coffee and bread and butter in the morning. They prefer to ask simply for their early morning *caffè*, and with them breakfast is *la colazione*. It is in reality our lunch. The lively Gaul's *déjeuner à la fourchette* is also lunch, and not literally the breaking of a fast. Stay: the Spaniards rightly give the name of *desayuno* to the matutinal cup of chocolate, corrected by a glass of cold water and a crust of bread; but, on the other hand, the Anglo-Indian's first meal of tea or coffee, with a little bread and butter, or bread and jam, generally brought to the bedside between five and six in the morning, is known as *chotahazri*, which means 'little breakfast.' A big breakfast, comprising various curries, follows at ten, to be succeeded at two p.m. by a copious tiffin; but at this repast, and at the dinner, which takes place at seven or eight, it is no longer good form, in smart Anglo-Indian society, to serve curry.

English people eat, as a rule, a great deal too much meat and not half enough vegetables. The Australians are literally gorgers of beef and mutton; and it is an equally common and painful spectacle to see a little New South Wales or a Victorian child devouring mutton chops or rump steaks at eight or nine o'clock in the morning. The Americans are quite as great sinners in this respect; and small Miss

Columbia or diminutive Master Birdofreedom Saurin will think nothing of 'wolfing' pork-steak, tenderloin steak, and mutton cutlets, after the hominy or the crushed wheat, and prior to the buckwheat cakes soaked in butter and drenched with maple syrup. Our transatlantic cousins have also an unholy fondness for fried potatoes at breakfast-time. Of their equally passionate liking for hot bread I will say nothing; because we also in this country have a *penchant* for hot buttered toast and hot French rolls. I had a friend once who prided himself on the possession of a cook unequalled in the invention of breakfast dishes. One of these devices was to send half a pound of prime Epping or Cambridge sausages to the family baker, and request him to insert the sausages in the dough or as many rolls. They came home smoking, and saturated with the grease from the porcine compost. My friend went to Rome; and I learned that he succeeded in persuading the people at Nazzari's restaurant, in the Piazza di Spagna, to supply muffins with anchovies inside them. This fanatic of the breakfast-table died early, and lies buried in the Protestant cemetery at Rome hard by the pyramid of Caius Cestius.

The Thorough Good Cook, 1895

The Incompleat Teetotaller

The Compleat Imbiber has ever been magnanimous, and previous volumes have included such teetotal masterpieces as the Victorian ballad *O, Come With Me to the Fountain, Love*! and, to especially loud acclaim from readers, William McGonagall's *Tribute to Mr Murphy and the Blue Ribbon Army* and his autobiographical fragment, *The First Man Who Threw Peas At Me Was a Publican*.

But now, alas, research unmasks Dundee's Poet and Tragedian for the hypocrite that he was. Compare, dear reader, the two poems that follow:

A New Temperance Poem in Memory of My Departed Parents, Who Were Sober Living & God Fearing People

My parents were sober living, and often did pray,
For their family to abstain from intoxicating drink alway;
Because they knew it would lead them astray,
Which no God fearing man will dare to gainsay.

Some people do say that God made strong drink,
But he is not so cruel I think;
To lay a stumbling block in his children's way,
And then punish them for going astray.

No! God has more love for his children, than mere man.
To make strong drink their souls to damn;
His love is more boundless than mere man's by far,
And to say not it would be an unequal par.

A man that truly loves his family wont allow them to drink,
Because he knows seldom about God they will think,
Besides he knows it will destroy their intellect,
And cause them to hold their parents in disrespect.

Strong drink makes the people commit all sorts of evil,
And must have been made by the Devil
For to make them quarrel, murder, steal, and fight,
And prevent them from doing what is right.

The Devil delights in leading the people astray,
So that he may fill his kingdom with them without delay;
It is the greatest pleasure he can really find,
To be the enemy of all mankind.

The Devil delights in breeding family strife,
Especially betwixt man and wife;
And if the husband comes home drunk at night,
He laughs and crys, ha! ha! what a beautiful sight.

And if the husband asks his supper when he comes in,
The poor wife must instantly find it for him;
And if she cannot find it, he will curse and frown,
And very likely knock his loving wife down.

Then the children will scream aloud,
And the Devil no doubt will feel very proud,
If he can get the children to leave their own fireside,
And to tell their drunken father, they won't with him reside.

Strong drink will cause the gambler to rob and kill his brother,
Aye! also his father and his mother,
All for the sake of getting money to gamble,
Likewise to drink, cheat, and wrangle.

And when the burglar wants to do his work very handy,
He plies himself with a glass of Whisky, Rum, or Brandy,
To give himself courage to rob and kill,
And innocent people's blood to spill.

Whereas if he couldn't get Whisky, Rum, or Brandy,
He wouldn't do his work so handy;
Therefore, in that respect let strong drink be abolished in time,
And that will cause a great decrease in crime.

Therefore, for this sufficient reason remove it from society,
For seldom burglary is committed in a state of sobriety;
And I earnestly entreat ye all to join with heart and hand,
And to help to chase away the Demon drink from bonnie Scotland.

I beseech ye all to kneel down and pray,
And implore God to take it away;
Then this world would be a heaven, whereas it is a hell,
And the people would have more peace in it to dwell.

and yet

The Heatherblend Club Banquet

'Twas on the 16th of October, in 1894,
I was invited to Inverness, not far from the seashore,
To partake of a Banquet prepared by the Heatherblend Club,
Gentlemen who honoured me without any hubbub.

The Banquet was held in the Gellion Hotel,
And the landlord, Mr Macpherson, treated me right well;
Also the servant maids were very kind to me,
Especially the girl who polished my boots most beautiful to see.

The Banquet consisted of roast beef, potatoes, and red wine,
Also hare soup and sherry, and grapes most fine,
And baked pudding and apples, lovely to be seen,
Also rich sweet milk and delicious cream.

Mr Gossip, a noble Highlander, acted as chairman,
And when the Banquet was finished the fun began;
And I was requested to give a poetic entertainment,
Which I gave, and which pleased them to their hearts' content.

And for the entertainment they did me well reward
By entitling me the Heatherblend Club Bard;
Likewise I received an Illuminated Address,
Also a purse of silver, I honestly confess.

Mr A. J. Stewart was very kind to me,
And tried all he could to make me happy;
And several songs were sung by gentlemen there—
It was the most social gathering I've been in, I do declare.

*   *   *

I wish the Heatherblend members every success,
Hoping God will prosper them and bless;
Long May Dame Fortune smile upon them,
For all of them I've met are kind gentlemen.

And, in conclusion, I must say
I never received better treatment in my day
Than I received from my admirers in bonnie Inverness;
This on my soul and conscience I do confess.

*   *   *

Oh, fie! sweet singer of Dundee —
I must wag a chiding finger or two at thee:
Thou hast written many a sanctimonious line
About the dangers of imbibing any sort of intoxicating liquor such
*   as wine*
And yet seem happy to have been made merry
On the Heatherblend Club's roast beef, potatoes, red wine, hare
*   soup and sherry ...*

What to Buy and What to Drink in 1987

Edmund Penning-Rowsell

o the issues of *The Compleat Imbiber* between 1961 and 1970 I contributed eight articles on the above theme; leafing through them again one is bound to notice how the conditions have changed for buying fine wines.

Even allowing for inflation, the top wines have become more expensive; there is now much bigger initial demand, particularly from America; an investment speculation element exists hardly known in the early 'sixties; and merchants at all levels can no longer afford to hold the stocks of vintage wine that they were expected to and previously did.

Bearing in mind that the 1960 pound is now worth only about 13 pence and the 1970 one less than 20 pence – roughly a seventh and a fifth respectively – most fine vintage wines are not more costly than they were when first offered, with the exception of first-growth clarets, vintage port and probably a few top red and white burgundies. In *The Compleat Imbiber* No. 4 (1961) it was stated that we would have to pay 'the better part of £2 a bottle' for Mouton Rothschild 1959, i.e. less than £24 a case. But for the year-old 1984 we would be lucky to have laid out less than £325 a dozen by the time, duty and VAT included, it reached our cellars. The celebrated 1963 ports opened at around £12 a dozen, whereas the 1983s were first offered at about £145 delivered. The difference today lies, however, with almost all fine wines, in that after the opening the prices rise much more quickly and sharply than they did.

This has partly been brought about by the other changes mentioned already. North America, particularly the USA with its immense buying power, only seriously took to drinking fine wines in the early to middle 'sixties, and went heavily on what they call 'futures' – thus putting wine on the same level as cotton or wheat. The 1970 was the first claret year that attracted them on a large scale.

Today it is estimated that about 70 per cent of first-growth clarets cross the Atlantic as a result of early offers, and a good percentage of the lesser classed growths. Americans also buy a large proportion of the white burgundies – hence their present generally very high prices.

However, buying for investment and speculation, which drives up the price of perhaps 50 celebrated classed-growth clarets and then indirectly pushes up the price of lesser growths, is much more a European, especially a British, affair, if only because it is much easier to re-sell wines at auction here than it is in the United States. There always has been speculation in wine, chiefly in the trade, but it began for individuals and companies when inflation began to bite in the 'sixties. In *The Imbiber* No. 4, 'a small but steady trickle of private money into wine' was reported, but it became much more significant at the end of the 'sixties and 'seventies. Not only does it put up prices but it makes the top wines very scarce. So, by the autumn of 1985, Lafite 1982, the ex-château opening price of which in the summer of 1983 had been 170 fcs. a bottle was costing 575 fcs. on the Bordeaux market, while Pétrus, the initial price of which was the same as Lafite's, sold at Christies for £2,500 a case – more than £200 a bottle, and still far from drinkable. But then no American cellar of distinction can afford to be without Pétrus, of which no more than 4,000 cases are made in an average year.

The final change in the last fifteen years or so that must influence our wine-buying policy is the inability of the trade, at source and in Britain, to hold and mature stocks. So growers and merchants in the wine-growing regions of Europe try to sell their new young wines as quickly as possible to retail merchants round the world, and these in turn pass as much of them on as soon as they can: not only fine clarets and burgundies but comparatively minor wines from these regions, as well as Rhônes, German wines and, of course, ports.

That is the background against which we should plan our purchases for 1987. Here we need not concern ourselves with any but superior wines, for there is no lack of excellent, reasonably-priced wines available for immediate drinking: Beaujolais, white wines from the Loire, medium-quality Rhônes, middle-range Germans and easy-drinking Italians. And nowadays we can go further abroad to Australia, New Zealand and, if rather more expensively, to the U.S.A.

As nowadays we have to buy vintage wines much earlier than in the not so distant past, we should first ask ourselves what is our annual consumption of such wines likely to be, and where are we going to keep them until they are ready to drink?

Vintage port apart, the wines that probably call for most prolonged keeping are clarets, although there is a vast difference between leading classed-growths and *petits châteaux*: the former may not reach their peak for 20 years or more, while the latter may be somewhere near their best after four or five. All depends on the vintage. Comparatively few of us are in a position, physically or financially, to keep, say, the 1985 classed Médocs well into the first decade of the coming century, but there is at least a good case for following the old Bordeaux tradition of not drawing the cork on fine clarets until they are a minimum of ten years old. So before buying clarets '*en primeur*' it is worth trying to estimate when we hope to drink them. This also will relate to what we already possess; and there are other wines that require ageing that we may wish to buy: red burgundy and Rhônes are the most immediate alternatives. Most of these are drinkable younger than fine clarets, though *grand cru* red burgundies may develop for well over ten years, and so will such top northern Rhônes as Hermitage and Côte-Rôtie.

The facilities for keeping young, immature vintage wines are of great importance; they have probably cost a fair amount of money and deserve to be drunk in good shape. The ideal is, of course, a dark cellar with a relatively constant temperature of 13°C (55°F), although a temperature that varies gradually with the seasons but does not go to extremes is satisfactory. Not many, however, enjoy such conditions; nor a north-facing pantry, as is sometimes recommended, while the other alternative of a store under the stairs is not suitable for long-term keeping. So without a suitable domestic solution to the problem, the best course is to store with a wine merchant who offers proper keeping facilities. Therefore, failing domestic accommodation in one's home or in a friend's, one should buy only the kind of wines that we are discussing from merchants who can keep 'customers' reserves'. The current level of rents is about £3 – £3.50 a case per year including VAT; not expensive for the security offered. It is worth making sure that one's wine is separately identified in the firm's cellars and books, so that if anything goes wrong with the company the receiver does not add your wine to the creditor's assets. This has happened in the past.

So what do we buy in 1987?

Assuming that we are starting fresh, and we have nothing much in reserve, the best claret vintage to buy for drinking not too far ahead is the 1981: elegant, classical-style clarets that have been over-shadowed by the greatly publicised 1982s and the rather less loudly acclaimed 1983s.

Clearly every claret amateur should have both vintages in the cellar, but largely because of investment and American demand they are expensive, particularly the 1982s. For those with relatively limited budgets the best bets might be the *crus bourgeois* of both years. Although 1982 has had more publicity than 1983 there are those who believe that in some cases more balanced wine was produced by some châteaux in the latter year.

Nor should 1984 be ignored by those with reserves of older years. It was one of those vintages, like 1980, that, because of a poor summer, was damned before the grapes were picked. Certainly it was a disaster for the Merlot grape, and therefore for St Emilion and Pomerol, but some very sound wines were made in the Médoc and the Graves. Unfortunately many of the classed growths, except the firsts, raised their opening prices with the excuse of a small crop. The 1984s are expected to mature more rapidly than the 1982s and 1983s, and those who possess them may be glad to have wines to open before these finer vintages.

There is no call to buy dry white Bordeaux in advance, except for the wines of the few Graves châteaux, among them Haut-Brion Blanc, Laville Haut-Brion and Domaine de Chevalier, that make exceptional, but also very expensive wines. A newcomer in this class is the Pavillon Blanc de Château Margaux, now produced with much more care than in the past. For sweet white Bordeaux the year to buy is 1983, rich and luscious. In 1985 it was too hot and dry to produce the 'noble rot' (*botrytis cynerea*) that inspires these wines.

Buying burgundy presents problems of price as well as of vintage. The crops are a fraction of those in the leading districts of the Gironde, and successful vintages less frequent: say three in a decade rather than five. So, with a world-wide demand, they are distinctly expensive. The best recent vintages to buy are 1978, 1980, 1982 (in part), 1983 and 1985. The best value in the circumstances are not the top Grands Crus such as Chambertin, Musigny or Volnay Caillerets, but the lesser single vineyards of Nuits-St Georges, Savigny and Santenay from a reliable source, or the village wines, Gevrey-Chambertin or Chambolle Musigny. Much less expensive, but also produced from the Pinot Noir grape are the Chalonnais wines, Givry, Rully and Mercurey. They are lighter and develop much more quickly than the Côte d'Or wines, which usually need from seven to ten years.

With the present fashion everywhere for white wines, the demand for white burgundies has reached almost a pitch of frenzy. In the Côte d'Or they account, in the leading villages of Puligny, Chassagne, Meursault and Aloxe, for only a quarter of the total production. Chablis, further north, is particularly subject to frost as well as hail. The Chalonnais and Mâconnais are less at risk, but owing to American demand, Pouilly Fuissé now costs as much as, if not more than, Meursault, which is ridiculous. The vintages for buying, if one can secure them, are 1981, 1983, and 1984 (moderate) and 1985. Of all fine French wines they are among the earliest to be available for drinking; and, in spite of the Australian and California Chardonnays, a fine Puligny or Meursault is *hors concours.*

Owing both to improved production and the high price of red burgundies, the Rhône reds have increasingly come on to the laying-down list. There is a more consistent level of vintage quality north of Lyons, although there are variations between the Northern Rhône, renowned for Hermitage and Côte-Rôtie, followed by Crozes-Hermitage, the quality of which depends very much on the grower or merchant, and the Southern Rhône, centred on Avignon and Orange; with Châteauneuf-du-Pape as the wine for keeping. Vintages to buy are 1980, for drinking now, 1982 (in the north), 1983, a great year and 1985, also exceptional. Most Rhône reds of quality are drunk too young. A great Hermitage may develop for 20 years and more, and a good Châteauneuf deserves ten.

Alsace wines are also often opened far too young. Protected by the Vosges mountains, they have a high proportion of good vintages. Whereas until a few years ago there was only one basic Alsace *appellation controlée*, there is now a higher, restricted Grand Cru appellation based on selected sites. The best vintages still available are 1981, 1983 (exceptional) and 1985.

The same mistake of premature drinking applies to the fine estate wines of the Moselle and Rhine in good years. Even moderate years like 1979 and 1981 improve with some bottle age, while an outstanding vintage like 1983 in the Kabinett Auslese range calls for at least six or seven years' maturing. This applies above all to the Rieslings.

Mistakenly, few in Britain would consider any Italian wines for buying for anything but immediate drinking and at low prices too. Some of the leading wines, such as Antinori's Tignanello and Lungarotti's Torgiano, are not released until ready for drinking but other, like Barolo and Barbaresco, which legally may be marketed after only three and two years respectively are well worth picking up then at remarkably moderate prices and put away for anything up to ten to twelve years. The best recent available vintage for these Piedmontese wines are 1978 and 1982.

Finally, for the buying budget, vintage port. The most recent vintages are well enough known: 1977, 1980, 1982 (declared by only a few houses) and 1983 (a small crop); 1977 is now generally regarded as the finest vintage since 1963, and every port drinker should have some, though they are now growing expensive. The 1980s and 1982s are regarded as of lesser quality, but the generally declared 1983 s are thought more important and should be snapped up, for a market is developing in the U.S.A. for laying down young vintage port.

It is always easier to recommend vintage wines for drinking than for buying, as the quality can generally then be seen, although with claret in particular it is more difficult to know when the more important châteaux will be at their best. One thing is almost certain: they will probably take longer to develop than is expected, and then longer before they go down than feared. With the exception of a few 1961s all the vintages of the 'sixties and some of the 'seventies should be drinkable. The exceptions are 1970, 1975, 1978 and some 1979s. Delicious easy-to-drink clarets were produced in 1980, and it may not be long before the 1981s are 'worth looking at', as that encouraging phrase has it. Indeed the lesser growths already are.

Among red burgundies all the 'sixties are for drinking, although some 1966s and 1969s have plenty of body. Among the 'seventies the only one to hold back is 1978, which does not mean, of course, that the 1976s and 1979s lack life. It all depends on how and by whom the wines were made, and for this we must rely on a reliable wine merchant. Like other fine white wines, white burgundies are generally drunk too young, with the Côte d'Or wines benefiting most from keeping, while all but top class chablis, the Chalonnais whites, Montagny and Rully, and the Macons, including Pouilly Fuissé, will probably be at their best after about three years. The best years for drinking the Côte d'Or whites are 1978, and 1979 and

1981, while the 1983s and the 1985s should be kept.

As for the red Rhônes the differences between south and north make generalisation difficult. The vintage to keep is 1978; otherwise all between then and 1983 should be drinkable. According to quality, the whites are probably at their best for drinking at between two and five years old.

By 1987 the 1983 Alsace wines should be beginning to show their fine form, but there will be no hurry to drink them, particularly the Rieslings, the Alsatians' favourite, and the Gewurztraminers, Alsace's best seller.

What German wines to drink in 1987 depends very much on the grape and the district. Müller-Thurgau wines, especially those from the Rheinhesse, need to be drunk when young, but Rieslings from well-known estates in the Moselle, Rheingau, Nahe and Pfalz will show more quality if kept. Franconian wines are usually drunk fairly young. The 1981s should be at their peak, the Kabinett 1983s at least ready for sampling. The loveliest, most luscious vintage for drinking now is 1976.

All that can be said about the majority of Italian red wines and, for that matter, Spanish Riojas and Catalan wines, is that those listed by wine merchants are ready for drinking. Rioja Reservas are certainly worth going for, as they have to have a minimum of four years' age. Gran Reservas must be a year old and come from an accepted fine vintage.

That leaves port. The 1963s do not need recommending, nor do they require drinking. I still find 1960s delicious, although never highly regarded in the hierarchy. The best senior vintage for current consumption seems to be 1966, the youngest one the not so exciting 1975. Some of the most agreeable, and less expensive, vintage ports to drink are the single-quinta wines of generally undeclared years. They will include Taylor's Vargellas, Graham's Malvedos and Calem's Quinta de Foz. No less attractive is fine old tawny port, which is probably at its best around 20 years old. At 10 years it is too young, over 30 too old.

Although in looking for vintage wines to drink, one should not be dazzled by age – and with white wines more often than not warned against it – far more wine is drunk too young than too old. In *The Compleat Imbiber* No. 12 (1971) Robin Don, Master of Wine and wine-merchant, wrote 'if vintage port has a lesson for us all it is that to enjoy the better things of life it does not pay to be in a hurry'.

Notes on Some Contributors

Kingsley Amis, CBE: *b* 1922
Novelist and poet.
Contributor to *Compleat Imbiber* No. 2 (1958).
Recreations: Music, thrillers, television.

John Arlott, OBE: *b* 1914
Poet and sometime policeman.
Contributor to *Compleat Imbiber* No. 1 (1956). Hon. Life Member, MCC.
Recreations: Watching cricket, drinking wine, talking, sleeping, collecting aquatints, engraved glass and wine artefacts.

E.F. Benson: 1867–1940
Creator of Lucia and Miss Mapp.
'An uncontrollably prolific writer... his reminiscences have value as sources for social history'. (D.N.B.)

Julian Critchley, MP: *b* 1930
Conservative member for Aldershot.
Recreations: Watching boxing, the country, reading military history, looking at churches, collecting Staffordshire.

Elizabeth David, CBE, FRSL
Chevalier du Mérite Agricole (France); Grande dame of English writers on Food.
Contributor to *Compleat Imbiber* Nos. 5 (1962), 6 (1963), 7 (1964), 8 (1965).

Paul Dehn: 1912–76
Poet, critic, script-writer.
Contributor to *Compleat Imbiber* Nos. 2 (1958), 5 (1962).

The Hon. Peter Dickinson: *b* 1927
Writer of detective stories, childrens' books and light verse; Assistant Editor of *Punch* 1952–69.
Contributor to *Compleat Imbiber* Nos. 4 (1961), 6 (1963), 7 (1964), 9 (1967), 10 (1969), 12 (1971).
Recreation: Manual labour.

Christopher Driver: *b* 1932
Food and drink editor, *Guardian*; Editor, *The Good Food Guide*, 1969–82.
Recreations: Cooking, playing violin, and viola, fell walking, accumulating books as reader and dealer.

Gavin Ewart, FRSL: *b* 1916
Cholmondeley Award for Poetry 1971.
Recreations: Reading, listening to music.

Peter Fleming, OBE: 1907–71
Traveller; *Times* special correspondent; author; soldier.
Contributor to *Compleat Imbiber* No. 2 (1958).

Clement Freud, MP: *b* 1924
Liberal member for Cambridgeshire North-East; writer, broadcaster, caterer.
Recreations: Racing, backgammon.

Roy Fuller CBE, FRSL: *b* 1912
Solicitor and author.
Professor of Poetry, Oxford 1968–73.

General Sir John Hackett, GCB, CBE, DSO, MC, FRSL: *b* 1910
Soldier (cavalry and airborne) and classical scholar.
Sometime C-in-C British Army of the Rhine and President of the Classical Association.

The Rt. Hon. Roy Hattersley, MP: *b* 1932
Deputy Leader, the Labour Party; essayist (*Punch*, *Guardian*, etc).

Margaret Lane (Countess of Huntingdon): *b* 1907
Novelist, biographer, journalist; Prix Femina-Vie Heureuse, 1936; President, Johnson Society, Jane Austen Society; Past-President Brontë Society and Dickens Fellowship.

Bernard Levin: *b* 1928
Journalist and author; Hon. Fellow LSE; columnist, *The Times*; Past-President The English Association.

Sir Harry Luke, KCMG: 1884–1969
Colonial administrator, scholar, traveller, author.

Norman Lewis: *b* 1908
Novelist and travel-writer: ranged widely through Mediterranean, Balkan countries and Levant before and during the war.

Roger Lewis: *b* 1961
Junior Research Fellow in English, Wolfson College, Oxford.

William McGonagall: 1830–1902
Dundee hand-loom weaver.
'His naive and unscanned doggerel continues to entertain, and he now enjoys a reputation as the world's worst poet.' *Oxford Companion to English Literature*, 1985
Contributor to *Compleat Imbiber* Nos. 3 (1960) and 4 (1961).

William Somerset Maugham: 1874–1965
Novelist, short-story writer, playwright. In his own opinion, 'in the very first row of the second-raters'.

John Mortimer, QC: *b* 1923
Barrister, playwright and author.
Recreations: Working, gardening, going to opera.

Iris Murdoch, CBE: *b* 1919
Novelist and philosopher; Fellow of St Annes's College, Oxford. First in Greats 1942; James Tait Black Memorial Prize 1973; Whitbread Prize 1974; Booker Prize 1978. *m* John Bayley, Professor of English Literature, Oxford.
Recreation: Learning languages.
Contributor to *Compleat Imbiber* No. 2 (1958).

Edmund Penning-Rowsell: *b* 1913
Wine correspondent, *Financial Times* and *Country Life*; Chairman, Wine Society.
Recreations: Opera and William Morris.
Contributor to *Compleat Imbiber* Nos. 4 (1961), 5 (1962), 6 (1963), 7 (1964), 8 (1965), 9 (1967), 10 (1969), 11 (1970).

Elizabeth Ray: *b* 1925
Social worker, magistrate, Home Office Prison Visitor, Director of Kent Opera, cookery correspondent, *Observer* 1969–74, and to various magazines.
Author of four cookery books. *m* Cyril Ray 1953.
Contributor to *Compleat Imbiber* Nos. 11 (1970), 12 (1971).

Elizabeth Romer
Studied textile design at the Royal College of Art; worked for the German Archaeological Institute at Cairo recording private Theban tombs.
Married to TV archaeologist John Romer.
Lives in Tuscany.

George Augustus Sala: 1828–96
Journalist, war correspondent (*Illustrated London News*, *Daily Telegraph*).

Ruth Silvestre
Singer and actress (leading lady in *Man of La Mancha*). Restored, with husband, derelict farmhouse in Lot-et-Garonne while 'resting' in 1976.

Edith Templeton: *b* 1916
Educated in Prague and Paris; novelist and travel-writer. Lives in Italy.
Recreation: 'Travel, with the greatest comfort possible'.

Keith Waterhouse: *b* 1929
Member Punch Table; novelist, playwright, script-writer, columnist. Granada Columnist of the Year Award 1970; IPC Descriptive Writer of the Year Award 1970; IPC Columnist of the Year Award 1973; British Press Awards Columnist of the Year Award 1978; Granada Special Quarter-Century Award 1982. Eighteen books include *Mrs Pooter's Diary* 1983, *Collected Letters of a Nobody*, 1986.
Recreation: Lunch.

Roger Woddis: *b* 1917
Parodist and poet, regular light-versifier for *Punch*, *New Statesman* etc.

Robin and Judith Yapp
Dentist and doctor respectively; Robin, with his late doctor brother, founded the firm of Yapp Brothers in Mere, Wiltshire, in 1969, specialising in the wines of the Rhône and the Loire, with which they had fallen in love as undergraduates, cycling through France.
Recreations: Music, especially opera, collecting contemporary art, writing.

The Editor is indebted to *Who's Who* for much of the above information, 'Recreations' in particular.

The Illustrators

Some chapter headings and tailpieces in this collection are by Edward Ardizzone and Asgeir Scott (also responsible for the decorative borders), by kind permission of Harveys of Bristol, from their book of collected *Wine-List Decorations, 1961–3*.

Most of the other illustrations, apart from a few by Thackeray and V'S. Gilbert, are from *La Comédie de Notre Temps* (1874) and *La Vigne: Voyage Autour des Vins de France* (1878), written and illustrated by 'Bertall'.

The pseudonym, suggested by his patron, Balzac, is a near-anagram of the second forename of Charles Albert d'Arnoux (1820–82), a less well-known but not undistinguished contemporary of such brilliant French illustrators as Gavarni, Eugène Lami, Constantin Guys and Daumier. Better artists still – Courbet, Pissarro and Renoir – were on the other side of the Paris barricades when Bertall took up arms against the Commune in 1871.

The two illustrations on pp. 181, 188 are by Elizabeth Romer herself from her book *A Tuscan Year* and are reproduced here with her kind permission.

Acknowledgements

A Vintner's View... by kind permission of Anthony Berry, Director and former Chairman, Berry Brothers and Rudd Ltd.

...And a Diner's Out by kind permission of Edith Templeton and Methuen London.

Mrs Beeton and Mrs Dickens by kind permission of the Countess of Huntingdon.

The Sixty-Year-Old Solitary by kind permission of Mrs John Bayley, CBE.

Bingo for Bifteck by kind permission of Ruth Silvestre.

Sherry: A Story by kind permission of Nicholas Fleming.

Beats to the Bar, How to Succeed at the Bar, Pasta? Basta!, Wine and/or Women, Liberal sees Red, Good Health! by kind permission of the editor of *Punch*.

Have It Your Way, Madame Poulard's Secret by kind permission of Elizabeth David C BE.

Mouton, 1918 by kind permission of Baron Philippe de Rothschild.

'I Like All Simple Things' by kind permission of the executors of the estate of W. Somerset Maugham and William Heinemann Ltd.

How To Do It by kind permission of Norman Lewis.

The Boom in Beaumes. by kind permission of Robin and Judith Yapp.

Wine in General by kind permission of General Sir John Hackett, GCB, DSO, MC.

It Isn't Only Peaches Down in Georgia by kind permission of Peter Luke, MC.

Victorian Dinner-Party and quotations in *As a Sort of Hors d'Oeuvre* by kind permission of the estate of E.F. Benson and the Hogarth Press.

Corporate Luncheon by kind permission of Roy Fuller CBE. Published in *Subsequent to Summer* by The Salamander Press.

Drinker to Lover, Drunkard to Lecher and *McGonagall-type Triolet* by kind permission of Gavin Ewart and Century Hutchinson Ltd.

Returning to the Sauce by kind permission of Bernard Levin.

Two Harvests in Tuscany by kind permission of Elizabeth Romer from *A Tuscan Year* published by Weidenfeld & Nicolson Ltd.